COMPETITIVENESS

An International Economics Reader

FOREIGN AFFAIRS

NEW YORK

CONTENTS

THE COMPETITIVENESS DEBATE

TWO VIEWS ON TRADE WITH JAPAN

Competitiveness:
A Dangerous Obsession

Paul Krugman

THE HYPOTHESIS IS WRONG

IN JUNE 1993, Jacques Delors made a special presentation to the leaders of the nations of the European Community, meeting in Copenhagen, on the growing problem of European unemployment. Economists who study the European situation were curious to see what Delors, president of the EC Commission, would say. Most of them share more or less the same diagnosis of the European problem: the taxes and regulations imposed by Europe's elaborate welfare states have made employers reluctant to create new jobs, while the relatively generous level of unemployment benefits has made workers unwilling to accept the kinds of low-wage jobs that help keep unemployment comparatively low in the United States. The monetary difficulties associated with preserving the European Monetary System in the face of the costs of German reunification have reinforced this structural problem.

It is a persuasive diagnosis, but a politically explosive one, and everyone wanted to see how Delors would handle it. Would he dare tell European leaders that their efforts to pursue economic justice have produced unemployment as an unintended by-product? Would he admit that the EMS could be sustained only at the cost of a recession and face the implications of that admission for European monetary union?

PAUL KRUGMAN is Professor of Economics at the Massachusetts Institute of Technology. His most recent book is *Peddling Prosperity: Economic Sense and Nonsense in the Age of Diminished Expectations* (W. W. Norton).

Guess what? Delors didn't confront the problems of either the welfare state or the EMS. He explained that the root cause of European unemployment was a lack of competitiveness with the United States and Japan and that the solution was a program of investment in infrastructure and high technology.

It was a disappointing evasion, but not a surprising one. After all, the rhetoric of competitiveness—the view that, in the words of President Clinton, each nation is "like a big corporation competing in the global marketplace"—has become pervasive among opinion leaders throughout the world. People who believe themselves to be sophisticated about the subject take it for granted that the economic problem facing any modern nation is essentially one of competing on world markets—that the United States and Japan are competitors in the same sense that Coca-Cola competes with Pepsi—and are unaware that anyone might seriously question that proposition. Every few months a new best-seller warns the American public of the dire consequences of losing the "race" for the 21st century.[1] A whole industry of councils on competitiveness, "geo-economists" and managed trade theorists has sprung up in Washington. Many of these people, having diagnosed America's economic problems in much the same terms as Delors did Europe's, are now in the highest reaches of the Clinton administration formulating economic and trade policy for the United States. So Delors was using

---

[1] See, for just a few examples, Laura D'Andrea Tyson, *Who's Bashing Whom: Trade Conflict in High-Technology Industries,* Washington: Institute for International Economics, 1992; Lester C. Thurow, *Head to Head: The Coming Economic Battle among Japan, Europe, and America,* New York: Morrow, 1992; Ira C. Magaziner and Robert B. Reich, *Minding America's Business: The Decline and Rise of the American Economy,* New York: Vintage Books, 1983; Ira C. Magaziner and Mark Patinkin, *The Silent War: Inside the Global Business Battles Shaping America's Future,* New York: Vintage Books, 1990; Edward N. Luttwak, *The Endangered American Dream: How to Stop the United States from Becoming a Third World Country and How to Win the Geo-economic Struggle for Industrial Supremacy,* New York: Simon and Schuster, 1993; Kevin P. Phillips, *Staying on Top: The Business Case for a National Industrial Strategy,* New York: Random House, 1984; Clyde V. Prestowitz, Jr., *Trading Places: How We Allowed Japan to Take the Lead,* New York: Basic Books, 1988; William S. Dietrich, *In the Shadow of the Rising Sun: The Political Roots of American Economic Decline,* University Park: Pennsylvania State University Press, 1991; Jeffrey E. Garten, *A Cold Peace: America, Japan, Germany, and the Struggle for Supremacy,* New York: Times Books, 1992; and Wayne Sandholtz et al., *The Highest Stakes: The Economic Foundations of the Next Security System,* Berkeley Roundtable on the International Economy (BRIE), Oxford University Press, 1992.

a language that was not only convenient but comfortable for him and a wide audience on both sides of the Atlantic.

Unfortunately, his diagnosis was deeply misleading as a guide to what ails Europe, and similar diagnoses in the United States are equally misleading. The idea that a country's economic fortunes are largely determined by its success on world markets is a hypothesis, not a necessary truth; and as a practical, empirical matter, that hypothesis is flatly wrong. That is, it is simply not the case that the world's leading nations are to any important degree in economic competition with each other, or that any of their major economic problems can be attributed to failures to compete on world markets. The growing obsession in most advanced nations with international competitiveness should be seen, not as a well-founded concern, but as a view held in the face of overwhelming contrary evidence. And yet it is clearly a view that people very much want to hold—a desire to believe that is reflected in a remarkable tendency of those who preach the doctrine of competitiveness to support their case with careless, flawed arithmetic.

This article makes three points. First, it argues that concerns about competitiveness are, as an empirical matter, almost completely unfounded. Second, it tries to explain why defining the economic problem as one of international competition is nonetheless so attractive to so many people. Finally, it argues that the obsession with competitiveness is not only wrong but dangerous, skewing domestic policies and threatening the international economic system. This last issue is, of course, the most consequential from the standpoint of public policy. Thinking in terms of competitiveness leads, directly and indirectly, to bad economic policies on a wide range of issues, domestic and foreign, whether it be in health care or trade.

MINDLESS COMPETITION

MOST PEOPLE who use the term "competitiveness" do so without a second thought. It seems obvious to them that the analogy between a country and a corporation is reasonable and that to ask whether the United States is competitive in the world market

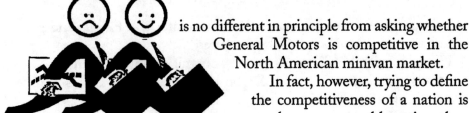

is no different in principle from asking whether General Motors is competitive in the North American minivan market.

In fact, however, trying to define the competitiveness of a nation is much more problematic than defining that of a corporation. The bottom line for a corporation is literally its bottom line: if a corporation cannot afford to pay its workers, suppliers, and bondholders, it will go out of business. So when we say that a corporation is uncompetitive, we mean that its market position is unsustainable—that unless it improves its performance, it will cease to exist. Countries, on the other hand, do not go out of business. They may be happy or unhappy with their economic performance, but they have no well-defined bottom line. As a result, the concept of national competitiveness is elusive.

A trade surplus may be a sign of national weakness, a deficit a sign of strength.

One might suppose, naively, that the bottom line of a national economy is simply its trade balance, that competitiveness can be measured by the ability of a country to sell more abroad than it buys. But in both theory and practice a trade surplus may be a sign of national weakness, a deficit a sign of strength. For example, Mexico was forced to run huge trade surpluses in the 1980s in order to pay the interest on its foreign debt since international investors refused to lend it any more money; it began to run large trade deficits after 1990 as foreign investors recovered confidence and began to pour in new funds. Would anyone want to describe Mexico as a highly competitive nation during the debt crisis era or describe what has happened since 1990 as a loss in competitiveness?

Most writers who worry about the issue at all have therefore tried to define competitiveness as the combination of favorable trade performance and something else. In particular, the most popular definition of competitiveness nowadays runs along the lines of the one given in Council of Economic Advisors Chairman Laura D'Andrea Tyson's *Who's Bashing Whom?:* competitiveness is "our ability to produce goods and services that meet the test of international competition while our citizens enjoy a standard of living that is both rising and sustainable." This sounds reasonable. If you think about it, however, and test your thoughts against the facts, you will find out that there is much less to this definition than meets the eye.

Consider, for a moment, what the definition would mean for an economy that conducted very little international trade, like the United States in the 1950s. For such an economy, the ability to balance its trade is mostly a matter of getting the exchange rate right. But because trade is such a small factor in the economy, the level of the exchange rate is a minor influence on the standard of living. So in an economy with very little international trade, the growth in living standards—and thus "competitiveness" according to Tyson's definition—would be determined almost entirely by domestic factors, primarily the rate of productivity growth. That's domestic productivity growth, period—not productivity growth relative to other countries. In other words, for an economy with very little international trade, "competitiveness" would turn out to be a funny way of saying "productivity" and would have nothing to do with international competition.

But surely this changes when trade becomes more important, as indeed it has for all major economies? It certainly could change. Suppose that a country finds that although its productivity is steadily rising, it can succeed in exporting only if it repeatedly devalues its currency, selling its exports ever more cheaply on world markets. Then its standard of living, which depends on its purchasing power over imports as well as domestically produced goods, might actually decline. In the jargon of economists, domestic growth might be outweighed by deteriorating terms of trade.[2] So "competitiveness" could

---

[2] An example may be helpful here. Suppose that a country spends 20 percent of its income on imports, and that the prices of its imports are set not in domestic but in foreign currency. Then if the country is forced to devalue its currency—reduce its value in foreign currency—by 10 percent, this will raise the price of 20 percent of the country's spending basket by 10 percent, thus raising the overall price index by 2 percent. Even if domestic *output* has not changed, the country's real *income* will therefore have fallen by 2 percent. If the country must repeatedly devalue in the face of competitive pressure, growth in real income will persistently lag behind growth in real output.

It's important to notice, however, that the size of this lag depends not only on the amount of devaluation but on the share of imports in spending. A 10 percent devaluation of the dollar against the yen does not reduce U.S. real income by 10 percent—in fact, it reduces U.S. real income by only about 0.2 percent because only about 2 percent of U.S. income is spent on goods produced in Japan.

turn out really to be about international competition after all.

There is no reason, however, to leave this as a pure speculation; it can easily be checked against the data. Have deteriorating terms of trade in fact been a major drag on the U.S. standard of living? Or has the rate of growth of U.S. real income continued essentially to equal the rate of domestic productivity growth, even though trade is a larger share of income than it used to be?

To answer this question, one need only look at the national income accounts data the Commerce Department publishes regularly in the *Survey of Current Business.* The standard measure of economic growth in the United States is, of course, real GNP—a measure that divides the value of goods and services produced in the United States by appropriate price indexes to come up with an estimate of real national output. The Commerce Department also, however, publishes something called "command GNP." This is similar to real GNP except that it divides U.S. exports not by the export price index, but by the price index for U.S. imports. That is, exports are valued by what Americans can buy with the money exports bring. Command GNP therefore measures the volume of goods and services the U.S. economy can "command"—the nation's purchasing power—rather than the volume it produces.[3] And as we have just seen, "competitiveness" means something different from "productivity" if and only if purchasing power grows significantly more slowly than output.

Well, here are the numbers. Over the period 1959-73, a period of vigorous growth in U.S. living standards and few concerns about international competition, real GNP per worker-hour grew 1.85 percent annually, while command GNP per hour grew a bit faster, 1.87 percent. From 1973 to 1990, a period of stagnating living standards, command GNP growth per hour slowed to 0.65 percent. Almost all (91 percent) of that slowdown, however, was explained by a decline in domestic productivity growth: real GNP per hour grew only 0.73 percent.

---

[3] In the example in the previous footnote, the devaluation would have no effect on real GNP, but command GNP would have fallen by two percent. The finding that in practice command GNP has grown almost as fast as real GNP therefore amounts to saying that events like the hypothetical case in footnote one are unimportant in practice.

Similar calculations for the European Community and Japan yield similar results. In each case, the growth rate of living standards essentially equals the growth rate of domestic productivity—not productivity relative to competitors, but simply domestic productivity. Even though world trade is larger than ever before, national living standards are overwhelmingly determined by domestic factors rather than by some competition for world markets.

Countries do not compete with each other the way corporations do.

How can this be in our interdependent world? Part of the answer is that the world is not as interdependent as you might think: countries are nothing at all like corporations. Even today, U.S. exports are only 10 percent of the value-added in the economy (which is equal to GNP). That is, the United States is still almost 90 percent an economy that produces goods and services for its own use. By contrast, even the largest corporation sells hardly any of its output to its own workers; the "exports" of General Motors—its sales to people who do not work there—are virtually all of its sales, which are more than 2.5 times the corporation's value-added.

Moreover, countries do not compete with each other the way corporations do. Coke and Pepsi are almost purely rivals: only a negligible fraction of Coca-Cola's sales go to Pepsi workers, only a negligible fraction of the goods Coca-Cola workers buy are Pepsi products. So if Pepsi is successful, it tends to be at Coke's expense. But the major industrial countries, while they sell products that compete with each other, are also each other's main export markets and each other's main suppliers of useful imports. If the European economy does well, it need not be at U.S. expense; indeed, if anything a successful European economy is likely to help the U.S. economy by providing it with larger markets and selling it goods of superior quality at lower prices.

International trade, then, is not a zero-sum game. When productivity rises in Japan, the main result is a rise in Japanese real wages; American or European wages are in principle at least as likely to rise as to fall, and in practice seem to be virtually unaffected.

It would be possible to belabor the point, but the moral is clear:

while competitive problems could arise in principle, as a practical, empirical matter the major nations of the world are not to any significant degree in economic competition with each other. Of course, there is always a rivalry for status and power—countries that grow faster will see their political rank rise. So it is always interesting to *compare* countries. But asserting that Japanese growth diminishes U.S. status is very different from saying that it reduces the U.S. standard of living—and it is the latter that the rhetoric of competitiveness asserts.

One can, of course, take the position that words mean what we want them to mean, that all are free, if they wish, to use the term "competitiveness" as a poetic way of saying productivity, without actually implying that international competition has anything to do with it. But few writers on competitiveness would accept this view. They believe that the facts tell a very different story, that we live, as Lester Thurow put it in his best-selling book, *Head to Head,* in a world of "win-lose" competition between the leading economies. How is this belief possible?

CARELESS ARITHMETIC

ONE OF THE REMARKABLE, startling features of the vast literature on competitiveness is the repeated tendency of highly intelligent authors to engage in what may perhaps most tactfully be described as "careless arithmetic." Assertions are made that sound like quantifiable pronouncements about measurable magnitudes, but the writers do not actually present any data on these magnitudes and thus fail to notice that the actual numbers contradict their assertions. Or data are presented that are supposed to support an assertion, but the writer fails to notice that his own numbers imply that what he is saying cannot be true. Over and over again one finds books and articles on competitiveness that seem to the unwary reader to be full of convincing evidence but that strike anyone familiar with the data as strangely, almost eerily inept in their handling of the numbers. Some examples can best illustrate this point. Here are three cases of careless arithmetic, each of some interest in its own right.

Trade Deficits and the Loss of Good Jobs. In a recent article published in Japan, Lester Thurow explained to his audience the importance of reducing the Japanese trade surplus with the United States. U.S. real wages, he pointed out, had fallen six percent during the Reagan and Bush years, and the reason was that trade deficits in manufactured goods had forced workers out of high-paying manufacturing jobs into much lower-paying service jobs.

This is not an original view; it is very widely held. But Thurow was more concrete than most people, giving actual numbers for the job and wage loss. A million manufacturing jobs have been lost because of the deficit, he asserted, and manufacturing jobs pay 30 percent more than service jobs.

Both numbers are dubious. The million-job number is too high, and the 30 percent wage differential between manufacturing and services is primarily due to a difference in the length of the workweek, not a difference in the hourly wage rate. But let's grant Thurow his numbers. Do they tell the story he suggests?

The key point is that total U.S. employment is well over 100 million workers. Suppose that a million workers were forced from manufacturing into services and as a result lost the 30 percent manufacturing wage premium. Since these workers are less than 1 percent of the U.S. labor force, this would reduce the average U.S. wage rate by less than 1/100 of 30 percent—that is, by less than 0.3 percent.

This is too small to explain the 6 percent real wage decline *by a factor of 20.* Or to look at it another way, the annual wage loss from deficit-induced deindustrialization, which Thurow clearly implies is at the heart of U.S. economic difficulties, is on the basis of his own numbers roughly equal to what the U.S. spends on health care every week.

Something puzzling is going on here. How could someone as intelligent as Thurow, in writing an article that purports to offer hard quantitative evidence of the importance of international competition to the U.S. economy, fail to realize that the evidence he offers clearly shows that the channel of harm that he identifies was *not* the culprit?

High Value-added Sectors. Ira Magaziner and Robert Reich, both now influential figures in the Clinton Administration, first reached a broad audience with their 1982 book, *Minding America's Business.* The book advocated a U.S. industrial policy, and in the introduction the authors offered a seemingly concrete quantitative basis for such a policy: "Our standard of living can only rise if (i) capital and labor increasingly flow to industries with high value-added per worker and (ii) we maintain a position in those industries that is superior to that of our competitors."

Economists were skeptical of this idea on principle. If targeting the right industries was simply a matter of moving into sectors with high value-added, why weren't private markets already doing the job?[4] But one might dismiss this as simply the usual boundless faith of economists in the market; didn't Magaziner and Reich back their case with a great deal of real-world evidence?

Well, *Minding America's Business* contains a lot of facts. One thing it never does, however, is actually justify the criteria set out in the introduction. The choice of industries to cover clearly implied a belief among the authors that high value-added is more or less synonymous with high technology, but nowhere in the book do any numbers compare actual value-added per worker in different industries.

Value Added Per Worker, 1988
(in thousands of dollars)

CIGARETTES	488
PETROLEUM REFINING	283
AUTOS	99
STEEL	97
AIRCRAFT	68
ELECTRONICS	64
ALL MANUFACTURING	66

Such numbers are not hard to find. Indeed, every public library in America has a copy of the *Statistical Abstract of the United States,* which each year contains a table presenting value-added and employment by industry in U.S. manufacturing. All one needs to do, then, is spend a few minutes in the library with a calculator to come up with a table that ranks U.S. industries by value-added per worker.

The table on this page shows selected entries from pages 740-744 of the 1991 *Statistical Abstract.* It turns out that the U.S. industries with really high value-added per worker are in sectors with very high ratios of capital to labor, like cigarettes and petroleum refining. (This was predictable: because capital-intensive industries must earn a normal return on large investments, they must charge prices that are a larger markup over labor costs than labor-intensive industries, which means that they

---

[4] "Value-added" has a precise, standard meaning in national income accounting: the value added of a firm is the dollar value of its sales, minus the dollar value of the inputs it purchases from other firms, and as such it is easily measured. Some people who use the term, however, may be unaware of this definition and simply use "high value-added" as a synonym for "desirable."

have high value-added per worker).
Among large industries, value-added per
worker tends to be high in traditional
heavy manufacturing sectors like steel
and autos. High-technology sectors
like aerospace and electronics turn
out to be only roughly average.

**Competitiveness advocates are eerily inept
in their handling of the numbers.**

This result does not surprise
conventional economists. High
value-added per worker occurs in sectors that are highly capital-
intensive, that is, sectors in which an additional dollar of capital buys
little extra value-added. In other words, there is no free lunch.

But let's leave on one side what the table says about the way the
economy works, and simply note the strangeness of the lapse by Magaziner and Reich. Surely they were not calling for an industrial policy
that would funnel capital and labor into the steel and auto industries
in preference to high-tech. How, then, could they write a whole book
dedicated to the proposition that we should target high value-added
industries without ever checking to see which industries they meant?

Labor Costs. In his own presentation at the Copenhagen summit,
British Prime Minister John Major showed a chart indicating that
European unit labor costs have risen more rapidly than those in the
United States and Japan. Thus he argued that European workers have
been pricing themselves out of world markets.

But a few weeks later Sam Brittan of the *Financial Times* pointed
out a strange thing about Major's calculations: the labor costs were not
adjusted for exchange rates. In international competition, of course,
what matters for a U.S. firm are the costs of its overseas rivals measured in dollars, not marks or yen. So international comparisons of
labor costs, like the tables the Bank of England routinely publishes,
always convert them into a common currency. The numbers presented by Major, however, did not make this standard adjustment.
And it was a good thing for his presentation that they didn't. As Brittan pointed out, European labor costs have not risen in relative terms
when the exchange rate adjustment is made.

If anything, this lapse is even odder than those of Thurow or Magaziner and Reich. How could John Major, with the sophisticated statistical resources of the U.K. Treasury behind him, present an analysis that failed to make the most standard of adjustments?

These examples of strangely careless arithmetic, chosen from among dozens of similar cases, by people who surely had both the cleverness and the resources to get it right, cry out for an explanation. The best working hypothesis is that in each case the author or speaker wanted to believe in the competitive hypothesis so much that he felt no urge to question it; if data were used at all, it was only to lend credibility to a predetermined belief, not to test it. But why are people apparently so anxious to define economic problems as issues of international competition?

THE THRILL OF COMPETITION

THE COMPETITIVE metaphor—the image of countries competing with each other in world markets in the same way that corporations do—derives much of its attractiveness from its seeming comprehensibility. Tell a group of businessmen that a country is like a corporation writ large, and you give them the comfort of feeling that they already understand the basics. Try to tell them about economic concepts like comparative advantage, and you are asking them to learn something new. It should not be surprising if many prefer a doctrine that offers the gain of apparent sophistication without the pain of hard thinking. The rhetoric of competitiveness has become so widespread, however, for three deeper reasons.

First, competitive images are exciting, and thrills sell tickets. The subtitle of Lester Thurow's huge best-seller, *Head to Head,* is "The Coming Economic Battle among Japan, Europe, and America"; the jacket proclaims that "the decisive war of the century has begun . . . and America may already have decided to lose." Suppose that the subtitle had described the real situation: "The coming struggle in which each big economy will succeed or fail based on its own efforts, pretty much independently of how well the others do." Would Thurow have sold a tenth as many books?

Second, the idea that U.S. economic difficulties hinge crucially on our failures in international competition somewhat paradoxically makes those difficulties seem easier to solve. The productivity of the average American worker is determined by a complex array of factors, most of them unreachable by any likely government policy. So if you accept the reality that our "competitive" problem is really a domestic productivity problem pure and simple, you are unlikely to be optimistic about any dramatic turnaround. But if you can convince yourself that the problem is really one of failures in international competition—that imports are pushing workers out of high-wage jobs, or subsidized foreign competition is driving the United States out of the high value-added sectors—then the answers to economic malaise may seem to you to involve simple things like subsidizing high technology and being tough on Japan.

Finally, many of the world's leaders have found the competitive metaphor extremely useful as a political device. The rhetoric of competitiveness turns out to provide a good way either to justify hard choices or to avoid them. The example of Delors in Copenhagen shows the usefulness of competitive metaphors as an evasion. Delors had to say something at the EC summit; yet to say anything that addressed the real roots of European unemployment would have involved huge political risks. By turning the discussion to essentially irrelevant but plausible-sounding questions of competitiveness, he bought himself some time to come up with a better answer (which to some extent he provided in December's white paper on the European economy—a paper that still, however, retained "competitiveness" in its title).

By contrast, the well-received presentation of Bill Clinton's initial economic program in February 1993 showed the usefulness of competitive rhetoric as a motivation for tough policies. Clinton proposed a set of painful spending cuts and tax increases to reduce the Federal deficit. Why? The real reasons for cutting the deficit are disappointingly undramatic: the deficit siphons off funds that might otherwise have been productively invested, and thereby exerts a steady if small drag on U.S. economic growth. But Clinton was able instead to offer a stirring patriotic appeal, calling on the nation to act now in order to make the economy competitive in the global market—with the implication that dire economic consequences would follow if the United States does not.

Many people who know that "competitiveness" is a largely meaningless concept have been willing to indulge competitive rhetoric precisely because they believe they can harness it in the service of good policies. An overblown fear of the Soviet Union was used in the 1950s to justify the building of the interstate highway system and the expansion of math and science education. Cannot the unjustified fears about foreign competition similarly be turned to good, used to justify serious efforts to reduce the budget deficit, rebuild infrastructure, and so on?

A few years ago this was a reasonable hope. At this point, however, the obsession with competitiveness has reached the point where it has already begun dangerously to distort economic policies.

THE DANGERS OF OBSESSION

THINKING AND SPEAKING in terms of competitiveness poses three real dangers. First, it could result in the wasteful spending of government money supposedly to enhance U.S. competitiveness. Second, it could lead to protectionism and trade wars. Finally, and most important, it could result in bad public policy on a spectrum of important issues.

During the 1950s, fear of the Soviet Union induced the U.S. goverment to spend money on useful things like highways and science education. It also, however, led to considerable spending on more doubtful items like bomb shelters. The most obvious if least worrisome danger of the growing obsession with competitiveness is that it might lead to a similar misallocation of resources. To take an example, recent guidelines for government research funding have stressed the importance of supporting research that can improve U.S. international competitiveness. This exerts at least some bias toward inventions that can help manufacturing firms, which generally compete on international markets, rather than service producers, which generally do not. Yet most of our employment and value-added is now in services, and lagging productivity in services rather than manufactures has been the single most important factor in the stagnation of U.S. living standards.

A much more serious risk is that the obsession with competitiveness will lead to trade conflict, perhaps even to a world trade war.

Most of those who have preached the doctrine of competitiveness have not been old-fashioned protectionists. They want their countries to win the global trade game, not drop out. But what if, despite its best efforts, a country does not seem to be winning, or lacks confidence that it can? Then the competitive diagnosis inevitably suggests that to close the borders is better than to risk having foreigners take away high-wage jobs and high-value sectors. At the very least, the focus on the supposedly competitive nature of international economic relations greases the rails for those who want confrontational if not frankly protectionist policies.

We can already see this process at work, in both the United States and Europe. In the United States, it was remarkable how quickly the sophisticated interventionist arguments advanced by Laura Tyson in her published work gave way to the simple-minded claim by U.S. Trade Representative Mickey Kantor that Japan's bilateral trade surplus was costing the United States millions of jobs. And the trade rhetoric of President Clinton, who stresses the supposed creation of high-wage jobs rather than the gains from specialization, left his administration in a weak position when it tried to argue with the claims of NAFTA foes that competition from cheap Mexican labor will destroy the U.S. manufacturing base.

Perhaps the most serious risk from the obsession with competitiveness, however, is its subtle indirect effect on the quality of economic discussion and policymaking. If top government officials are strongly committed to a particular economic doctrine, their commitment inevitably sets the tone for policy-making on all issues, even those which may seem to have nothing to do with that doctrine. And if an economic doctrine is flatly, completely and demonstrably wrong, the insistence that discussion adhere to that doctrine inevitably blurs the focus and diminishes the quality of policy discussion across a broad range of issues, including some that are very far from trade policy per se.

Consider, for example, the issue of health care reform, undoubtedly the most important economic initiative of the Clinton administration, almost surely an order of magnitude more important to U.S. living standards than anything that might be done about trade

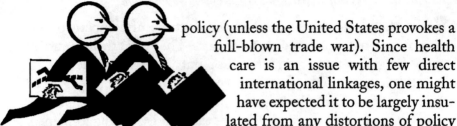

Competitiveness risks distorting the quality of domestic economic policy.

policy (unless the United States provokes a full-blown trade war). Since health care is an issue with few direct international linkages, one might have expected it to be largely insulated from any distortions of policy resulting from misguided concerns about competitiveness.

But the administration placed the development of the health care plan in the hands of Ira Magaziner, the same Magaziner who so conspicuously failed to do his homework in arguing for government promotion of high value-added industries. Magaziner's prior writings and consulting on economic policy focused almost entirely on the issue of international competition, his views on which may be summarized by the title of his 1990 book, *The Silent War.* His appointment reflected many factors, of course, not least his long personal friendship with the first couple. Still, it was not irrelevant that in an administration committed to the ideology of competitiveness Magaziner, who has consistently recommended that national industrial policies be based on the corporate strategy concepts he learned during his years at the Boston Consulting Group, was regarded as an economic policy expert.

We might also note the unusual process by which the health care reform was developed. In spite of the huge size of the task force, recognized experts in the health care field were almost completely absent, notably though not exclusively economists specializing in health care, including economists with impeccable liberal credentials like Henry Aaron of the Brookings Institution. Again, this may have reflected a number of factors, but it is probably not irrelevant that anyone who, like Magaziner, is strongly committed to the ideology of competitiveness is bound to have found professional economists notably unsympathetic in the past—and to be unwilling to deal with them on any other issue.

To make a harsh but not entirely unjustified analogy, a government wedded to the ideology of competitiveness is as unlikely to make good economic policy as a government committed to creationism is to make good science policy, even in areas that have no direct relationship to the theory of evolution.

ADVISERS WITH NO CLOTHES

IF THE OBSESSION with competitiveness is as misguided and damaging as this article claims, why aren't more voices saying so? The answer is, a mixture of hope and fear.

On the side of hope, many sensible people have imagined that they can appropriate the rhetoric of competitiveness on behalf of desirable economic policies. Suppose that you believe that the United States needs to raise its savings rate and improve its educational system in order to raise its productivity. Even if you know that the benefits of higher productivity have nothing to do with international competition, why not describe this as a policy to enhance competitiveness if you think that it can widen your audience? It's tempting to pander to popular prejudices on behalf of a good cause, and I have myself succumbed to that temptation.

As for fear, it takes either a very courageous or very reckless economist to say publicly that a doctrine that many, perhaps most, of the world's opinion leaders have embraced is flatly wrong. The insult is all the greater when many of those men and women think that by using the rhetoric of competitiveness they are demonstrating their sophistication about economics. This article may influence people, but it will not make many friends.

Unfortunately, those economists who have hoped to appropriate the rhetoric of competitiveness for good economic policies have instead had their own credibility appropriated on behalf of bad ideas. And somebody has to point out when the emperor's intellectual wardrobe isn't all he thinks it is.

So let's start telling the truth: competitiveness is a meaningless word when applied to national economies. And the obsession with competitiveness is both wrong and dangerous.✪

The Fight over Competitiveness

A Zero-Sum Debate?

Playing to Win

CLYDE V. PRESTOWITZ, JR.

Paul Krugman first achieved a measure of public recognition with a study of competition in the aircraft industry, which proved mathematically the potential efficacy of strategic—that is to say managed—trade. That this analysis was considered important might seem odd in view of the fact that the German-American scholar Friedrich List had done more or less the same work nearly 150 years ago and in view of the experience of the Japanese, who had been practicing strategic trade for more than 40 years at the time of Krugman's study. But given the narrow scope of the research considered permissible by the conventional wisdom of U.S. economists, as well as their ignorance of history and other disciplines, Krugman's analysis was a notable, iconoclastic achievement.

Indeed, it may have been too daring because ever since its publication Krugman has been running away from the implications of his own findings. His diatribe in *Foreign Affairs* (March/April) against the concept of competitiveness

and those who espouse it is only the most recent example.

Krugman not only claims that concern with competitiveness is misplaced. He attacks all those who think otherwise— including leading members of the Clinton administration such as Robert B. Reich, Ira C. Magaziner, Laura D'Andrea Tyson and the president himself—as protectionists whose work is careless if not dishonest and whose motives run from simple greed to chauvinism and demagoguery.

Krugman contends that concern about competitiveness is silly because as a practical matter the major countries of the world are not in economic competition with each other. He attempts to prove this by making three points. First he argues that trade is not a zero-sum game. Trade between the United States and Japan is not like competition between Coca-Cola and Pepsi because whereas Pepsi's gain is almost always Coke's loss, the United States and its trading partners can both be winners through the dynamics of comparative advantage.

Although true to some extent, this rationale ignores that different kinds of trade take place. Surely Krugman is cor-

rect in the case of trade between the United States and Costa Rica, where America imports bananas it does not grow and exports airplanes and machinery that Costa Rica does not make. Both countries come out winners by devoting their resources to what each does best. But what about the kind of trade typified by the recent Saudi Arabian order for $6 billion of new airplanes? Why were the Europeans so upset and Clinton so happy when the Saudis announced that U.S. producers would win all the orders? Both the Europeans and the Americans make airplanes, and this order means that the United States will gain jobs and income that Europe might have had but lost. This was largely a zero-sum trade situation, and ironically it was precisely the case that first brought Krugman to prominence. Maybe he was right the first time.

IT'S LIVING STANDARDS, STUPID

In fact, Krugman later concedes the point by allowing that "in principle" competitiveness problems could arise between countries. But he insists that they do not in practice because trade is a relatively small part of GNP in the major countries. Consequently, living standards are determined almost wholly by how well the economy works domestically rather than by international performance. In this vein, he observes that exports constitute only 10 percent of U.S. output, apparently leaving 90 percent of the economy to purely domestic factors. Moreover, he attributes 91 percent of the 1973 to 1990 stagnation in U.S. living standards to declining domestic productivity growth and only 9 percent to deteriorating terms of trade.

But competitiveness proponents have never denied the importance of domestic economic performance. Indeed, virtually all competitiveness prescriptions emphasize domestic savings and investment rates, education, cost of capital and research and development. Trade is typically treated as a secondary issue—more a symptom than a cause of subpar competitiveness. Second, Krugman ignores

America's imports—which equal 11 percent of GNP and nearly half of U.S. manufacturing output. Thus, overall trade is equivalent to about 21 percent of GNP, and by some estimates the impact of trade is felt directly by at least half the U.S. economy. Take the U.S. auto industry. It is not a big exporter, and imports account for only about 15 percent of the U.S. market. But the prices and quality of those imports help determine the retail prices U.S. automakers can charge, wages of U.S. auto workers and incomes of those who service the U.S. auto industry.

Krugman does not explain the slowdown in U.S. productivity growth, but he implies that domestic factors are the sole culprits. Yet the slowdown came just when U.S. imports were soaring and entire industries such as consumer electronics were being wiped out by foreign competitors pursuing mercantilist tactics. Surely these dislocations had some impact on U.S. productivity growth.

Krugman's third and final argument is that although countries may be rivals for status and power, such rivalry is something apart from economics and has no impact on living standards. A high relative growth rate may enhance Japan's status, for example, but it does not reduce the living standard of other countries. Although this notion may be true in the short-term, absolute sense, it is not necessarily true in the long-term, potential sense. Since the end of World War II, the United States has grown faster than Great Britain. The United States has done so in part by taking British inventions such as jet planes and radar and commercializing them faster than the British, thereby closing off those industries as potential avenues of British growth. Of course, if Britain could enter other high-growth, high-wage industries, the U.S. position would make no difference. But at any one time the number of those industries is limited; missing the boat on one can mean losing potential gains in living standards. In the extreme, loss of economic competitiveness can weaken national security and cause greater vulnerability to political regimes and international cartels that may severely constrain a country's economic potential. This competition is, after all, what imperialism and its opposition has been all about.

SPLITTING HAIRS

To buttress his arguments, Krugman attacks his critics' arithmetic as careless. Yet Krugman's own arithmetic is careless and selective. His analysis of how manufacturing job loss affects real average wages ignores the relationship between service and manufacturing wages. American barbers are not notably more productive than Bangladeshi barbers. But their wages are much higher because their customers work with much higher productivity than the customers of their Bangladeshi counterparts. Loss of high-wage U.S. manufacturing jobs also depresses not only manufacturing wages, but service industry wages as well. Krugman, however, fails to mention this drag.

Krugman's discussion of value added is even more questionable. He may have a point in that "high value added" has become a kind of shorthand for technology-intensive and high-wage industries when that is not always the case. But Krugman uses very broad industry categories to make his point, although the data he draws on clearly show that a huge industry like electronics consists of many sectors, some with high value added and others with low. Overall, Krugman notes a figure of value added per worker in the electronics industry of only $64,000. But why did he ignore the tables showing the figures of $443,000 for computers and $234,000 for semiconductors?

Krugman concludes by expressing fear of the possible distortion of the U.S. economy through the application of flawed competitiveness policies. He could, of course, be right. But can the United States be confident that an analyst who has such obvious gaps of his own and who has now argued both sides of the competitiveness issue can be relied on as the guide? Perhaps he is wrong, and competitiveness, far from being a dangerous obsession, is an essential concern.

CLYDE V. PRESTOWITZ, JR.

President of the Economic Strategy Institute and Director-General of the Pacific Basin Economic Council

Microchips, Not Potato Chips

LESTER C. THUROW

The Gang of Eight (Bill Clinton, John Major, Jacques Delors, Robert Reich, Laura D'Andrea Tyson, Mickey Kantor, Ira Magaziner, Lester Thurow) pleads not guilty to Paul Krugman's charges that it is grossly exaggerating the importance of international competitiveness.

Krugman asserts that, economically, nations have "no well-defined bottom

line." Wrong! Nations seek to raise the living standards of each citizen. Higher living standards depend on rising productivity, and in any economy the rate of productivity growth is principally determined by the size of domestic investments in plant and equipment, research and development, skills and public infrastructure, and the quality of private management and public administration.

I have written articles referring to strategic trade policies as the "seven percent solution." Ninety-three percent of economic success or failure is determined at home with only seven percent depending on competitive and cooperative arrangements with the rest of the world. My book, *The Zero-Sum Solution: Building a World-Class American Economy*, contains 23 pages on competitiveness issues, 45 pages on the importance of international cooperation and 333 pages on getting things right at home. The centrality of domestic invention and innovation is precisely why I agreed to lead the Lemelson-MIT program in invention and innovation, one part of which is a $500,000 prize for the American inventor and innovator of the year. The corpus of writings, speeches and actions of the rest of the Gang of Eight contains similar quotations, proportions and actions.

But remembering this sense of proportion, what is the role for competitiveness? Clearly something is wrong with Krugman's arithmetic that shows international trade cannot make much difference to American productivity. If his arithmetic were correct, then it follows that a lot of American protection might be quite a good thing.

Today 6 million Americans are working part-time who would like to work full-time, and almost 9 million are unemployed. In the last 20 years the bottom two-thirds of the male work force has taken a 20 percent reduction in real wages. The American work force could use a few million extra high-wage jobs. Suppose the United States were to impose quotas on manufactured imports so as to bring American imports (now 14 percent of gross domestic product) down to the 10 percent of GDP currently exported—that is, increase the domestically produced GDP by $250 billion. According to the U.S. Department of Commerce, if one divides manufacturing output by manufacturing employment, every $45 billion in extra output represents one million jobs. Production of current imports would absorb more than 5 million of those 15 million underemployed and unemployed people.

Since more Americans would be working in a sector with above-average productivity, national output and earnings would rise. The losses to the American consumer in the form of higher prices would be smaller than the gains to American producers in the form of higher earnings unless American producers were less than half as efficient as those abroad (an unlikely event). But even if that were the case, the economic burden of their inefficiency would be trivial relative to American GDP of $6.5 trillion. The gains to workers would be well worth the loss in output. But certainly none of the Gang of Eight advocates such policies, although they would seem to be called for by Krugman's simple arithmetic. Why?

WELCOME TO THE REAL WORLD

The simple arithmetic of what economists call "comparative statics" is technically right but economically wrong. If the domestic economy is to succeed in moving to higher levels of productivity and income, it must first compete successfully in the global economy. Foreign competition simultaneously forces a faster pace of economic change at home and produces opportunities to learn new technologies and new management practices that can be used to improve domestic productivity. Put bluntly, those who don't compete abroad won't be productive at home.

Although he denies saying it, Michael J. Boskin, chairman of President Bush's Council of Economic Advisers, will go down in history as the man who said, "It doesn't make any difference whether a country makes potato chips or computer chips!" The statement is wrong because wages and rates of return to capital are not everywhere equal.

The real world is in a perpetual state of dynamic disequilibrium where differentials in wages and rate of return to capital by industry are both large and persistent (these above-average wages or returns to capital are technically called disequilibrium quasi-rents). Within manufacturing in 1992 there was an almost four-to-one wage gap between those working in the highest- and lowest-paid industries. The industries at the top and bottom have changed little since World War II. Rates of return to capital similarly ranged from plus 27 percent in pharmaceuticals to minus 26 percent in building materials.

Pharmaceuticals top the rate of return charts every year. The market is always eliminating the high rates of return on existing drugs, but disequilibrium quasi-rents are always being created on new drugs. Because every successful pharmaceutical firm requires huge amounts of time and capital to build physical and human infrastructure, those already in the industry find it relatively easy to stay ahead of those who might seek to enter.

PUTTING PEOPLE FIRST

Those who lost jobs in autos and machine tools as American firms lost market share at home and abroad typically took a 30 to 50 percent wage reduction, if they were young. If they were over 50 years of age, they were usually permanently exiled to the periphery of the low-wage, part-time labor market. Their losses might not be a large faction of GDP, but those losses are important to the millions of affected workers and their families. The correct redress for their problems, however, is not to keep Japanese autos or machine tools out of the American market but to organize ventures such as the government-industry auto battery consortium that seeks to expand the American auto industry's market share by taking the lead in producing tomorrow's electric cars.

Since aircraft manufacturing generates technologies that later spread to the rest of the economy and above-average wages, the United States cannot simply ignore the government-financed European Airbus Industrie challenge in an industry America currently dominates.

The fastest-growing and technologically most exciting industry over the next decade is expected to be the industry that lies at the intersection of telecommunications, computers, television and the media arts. Given this prospect the United States cannot afford to let itself be locked out of the Japanese wireless telecommunications market or permit the Europeans to limit American movies and television programs to 40 percent of their markets. To do so is to make the entire American economy less dynamic and less technologically sophisticated and to generate lower American incomes than would otherwise be the case.

In the traditional theory of comparative advantage, Boskin and Krugman are correct. Natural resource endowments and factor proportions (capital-labor ratios) determine what countries should produce. Governments can and should do little when it comes to international competitiveness. With a world capital market, however, all now essentially borrow in London, New York or Tokyo regardless of where they live. There is no such thing as a capital-rich or capital-poor country. Modern technology has also pushed natural resources out of the competitive equation. Japan, with no coal or iron ore deposits, can have the best steel industry in the world.

This is now a much more dynamic world of brainpower industries and synthesized comparative advantage. Industries such as microelectronics, biotechnology, the new materials industries, telecommunications, civilian aircraft production, machine tools, and computer hardware and software have no natural geographic home. They will be located wherever someone organizes the brainpower to capture them. With man-made comparative advantage, one seeks not to find disequilibrium quasi-rents (the gold mine of yore) but to create the new products and processes that generate above-average wages and rates of return.

In their funding of education, skills and research and development, governments have an important role to play in organizing the brainpower necessary to create economic leadership. Just as military intelligence estimates about U.S.S.R. intentions partly guided yesterday's strategic military research and development, so the actions of U.S. economic competitors will partly guide tomorrow's civilian research and development. If the Japanese have an insurmountable lead in flat-screen video technology, it does not make sense to invest government or private resources or talent in a hopeless attempt to catch up.

The smart private firm benchmarks itself vis-à-vis its best domestic and international competition. Where it is not the world's best, it seeks to adopt the better practices found elsewhere. A smart country will do the same. Is America's investment in plant and equipment, research and development, skills and infrastructure world class? Do American managers, private and public, have something to learn from practices in the rest of the world? The purpose of such benchmarking is not to declare economic warfare on foreign competitors but to emulate them and elevate U.S. standards of performance.

Obsessions are not always wrong or dangerous. A passion for building a world-class economy that is second to none in generating a high living standard for every citizen is exactly what the United States and every other country should seek to achieve. Achieving that

goal in any one country in no way stops any other country from doing likewise.

LESTER C. THUROW
Professor of Management and Economics at the Alfred P. Sloan School of Management, Massachusetts Institute of Technology

Rule-Based Competition

RUDOLF SCHARPING

Professor Krugman has trained his sights on fellow economists and the political leaders they have influenced. To embrace skepticism and enlighten is the duty of a scientist, and Krugman does both. Politicians should not rely on explanations that give only one cause. In particular, theories that equate complex national economies with companies should be viewed with caution, especially if the emphasis on competition leads to a downgrading of social and environmental standards and coordinated economic policy.

It can be demonstrated that the level of prosperity of national economies depends to a large extent on the productivity and to a lesser extent on the international competitiveness of their companies. Because of its greater dependence on world markets, Germany is in a different situation than the United States. Germany's integration in the world economy has increased rapidly over the past decade. In addition, Germany is confronted with the singular problem of transforming the German Democratic Republic, a highly unproductive economy that was completely sealed off from international competition, into a productive market economy with open borders.

Nevertheless, Krugman suggests that even for a country as highly involved in foreign trade as Germany, the heavy burden of public debt, taxes and levies, and the thicket of regulations now pose a problem for investors and future productivity gains. Levies and regulations in Germany have reached such dimensions that they have a much greater impact than any adverse action by Japanese or American politicians.

In Germany as in any other country, those who follow the fashion of using international competitiveness to explain every economic problem risk making mistakes. The result is a waste of tax money or, worse, calls for closing borders. Even now, national economies are competing to cut taxes and offer industrial subsidies to increase investment and ease overheads, thus distorting market conditions. The result is rising public debt. At least this consequence has been the experience of the United States, which initiated the tax-cutting contest during the Reagan years.

Moreover, as a result of the global deregulation of the banking sector, an alarming trend has emerged. The money economy has taken on a life of its own. Government tax-cutting contests have produced a global market of tax evasion for financial assets. By comparison, investments in tangible fixed assets appear less profitable than making money directly with money, without taking the detour of producing goods. This shift in profit expectations is a major cause of increasing underemployment in many industrialized nations. It is a case of politically misdirected capital.

POLLUTING COMPETITION

In the contest for attracting or holding onto international companies, many governments are also cutting environmental regulations, which is detrimental to the future availability of natural factors of production. Of course, another result of this unfair competition is that the minimum social standards of the International Labour Organisation can be ignored with impunity.

The General Agreement on Tariffs and Trade had good reason to discuss environmental standards and free trade: to import goods from countries that are competitive only because they offer global resources free of charge has little to do with comparative cost advantages.

The ability of national economies to apply policy controls decreases with their interdependence with other economies. This becomes patently clear in fiscal policy when imports account for a high share of GNP. In these cases, it is questionable whether an expansive fiscal policy will stimulate domestic demand and generate additional tax revenues. Competing countries will delay their own stimulus until the former country has incurred the costs. The consequence of these waiting contests is clear: recessions in the world economy last longer than they would with a coordinated approach.

Since World War II, it has been common practice among the Western industrialized nations to avoid devaluation contests, and for good reason: such contests are harmful. They lead to beggar-thy-neighbor policies—extremely high public debt, consumption of resources and mass unemployment. Consequently, the public will no longer approve of an open world economy.

Competition requires rules; otherwise it will destroy itself. Competition without rules is unfair. For this reason, binding antitrust legislation has been adopted in the European Union. German politicians are in favor of strengthening the institutions of the European Union; and at least Germany's Social Democrats support the attempts made by European Commission President Jacques Delors to broaden the scope of fiscal and monetary policy for the highly integrated European economic area. Some conservative governments do not want to go beyond the creation of a single European market. Instead of coordinating economic policies multilaterally, they want the national economies to compete with one another in monetary and tax policies as well as in environmental and social standards. The potential winner of this competition is clear: internationally mobile capital. The likely loser is equally clear: the national economies. Krugman is right to warn that the exaggerated importance attached to competitiveness may lead to protectionism with all its prosperity-consuming evils.

There are many good reasons for promoting research and development, education and training, as well as technology at the national level to provide for future growth and employment at home. And one country can certainly learn from another how to increase productivity. However aggressive stances are not needed. If Krugman's article leads to a realization among political decision-makers that defining countries primarily as economic competitors is a mistake, it should result in greater international cooperation and policy coordination.

Rules are needed that do not completely preclude but nonetheless restrain unfair competition—among currencies, tax systems, industrial policy interventions as well as environmental and social standards. The world economic summits as well as informal meetings of the Group of Seven industrialized nations should regain the substance that they had in German Chancellor Helmut Schmidt's time. In view of the present global challenge, which all countries face in coping with structural change in a socially acceptable and ecologically sustainable manner, the industrialized nations must cooperate more closely, not only among themselves but with the developing countries.

RUDOLF SCHARPING
Chairman of the Social Democratic Party of Germany

Speaking Freely
STEPHEN S. COHEN

Paul Krugman contends that those who speak of competitiveness fail to understand three important points. First, nations are not like companies. No single number indicates their bottom line and the analogy does not apply. Second, he says that competitiveness is at best a meaningless concept. If it has any meaning whatever, it is "a poetic way of saying productivity." Productivity is the robust and unique measure of the performance of a national economy. Third, international trade is not a zero-sum game.

These are not stinging revelations but merely oft-repeated truisms. All his assertions are set out mundanely in The Report of the President's Commission on Competitiveness, written for the Reagan administration in 1984. The report provides what even Krugman acknowledges has become the standard definition:

> Competitiveness has different meanings for the firm and for the national economy ....A nation's competitiveness is the degree to which it can, under free and fair market conditions, produce goods and services that meet the test of international markets while simultaneously expanding the real incomes of its citizens. Competitiveness at the national level is based on superior productivity performance.

So all of Krugman's revelations are on page one of the basic text: no simple analogy equates a nation and a business, productivity lies at the center of competitiveness, and trade is not a zero-sum game; it can and should be free and fair.

What then, if anything, is Krugman flailing at? Nobody with whom Krugman should deign to take difference has ever said the silly things he pokes with his jousting spear. Lots of people vulgarize competitiveness, but that is true of just about every other idea in economics.

Krugman objects to President Clinton's likening of the U.S. economy to "a big corporation competing in the global marketplace." Presidential metaphors, which try to encapsulate complicated matters for purposes of political mobilization, have their own logic and history. Perhaps Clinton's simile is akin to Franklin D. Roosevelt's famous likening of the Lend-Lease Act to lending a neighbor a fire hose. Clinton was neither mendacious nor wrong. To remind Americans that in many ways they are all in this together is important, and in a

sense the national economy can be likened to a huge corporation—not big in the rude, trivializing example Krugman uses, Pepsi versus Coke, but big in the Mitsubishi, Mitsui or Sumitomo sense. The six main *keiretsu*—massive structures of grouped companies—which for many purposes come very close to being the Japanese economy, produce about half the Japanese total output of transportation equipment, banking, insurance, oil, glass, cement and shipping. Over one-half of all intermediate products are produced and bought within the cozy network of the six main groups, not to mention the lesser vertical *keiretsu*.

Lots of people, not just politicians, use "competitiveness" as a metaphor and do so a bit freely. Scientists talk of national competitiveness in biology; educators, in math. Part of the problem is the need for a single substantive term for "competitive position." Part is a heightened awareness, all to the good, that the United States is no longer supreme, benchmarking is a first step toward serious improvement, and comparative measures—even of economic welfare—have important and legitimate meanings.

Krugman criticizes those who write about competitiveness for their tendency to "engage in what may perhaps most tactfully be described as 'careless arithmetic.'" Yet Krugman's own arithmetic is, to say the least, careless. He provides a table that purports to demonstrate arithmetically that value-added production correlates not with technology but with capital intensity. But relating capital intensity to value added by sector contains a concealed correlation because the same table also ranks sectors by degree of monopoly power. And nothing generates more value added than monopoly. Furthermore, Krugman omitted at least one sector: pharmaceuticals. This sector should be number three on his list, with value added almost twice as high as autos. But value added in pharmaceuticals is not explained by lots of capital per worker; instead the pharmaceutical industry has lots of research per worker along with lots of sales effort and monopoly concentration. And for a more sophisticated understanding, one should look beyond production to sales figures in the United States, which include competition from imports. In cigarettes, the number-one industry in value added and number-one in monopoly concentration, competition from imports is trivial. That is a major reason for the high value added in cigarette production. But that raises big questions, such as what determines productivity? What operationally can and cannot be done with simple productivity numbers?

Krugman warns that an obsession with competitiveness is dangerous and advises cathecting onto productivity. A near-exclusive focus on productivity, however, has some particular dangers and problems. Competitiveness puts productivity at the center of its concerns but not as an explanation. Instead competitiveness points out that overall productivity rates, which are very complex syntheses, are the things to explain, and that economics does not know how to do that.

BEGGAR-THY-QUESTION

Krugman unwittingly illustrates the problem of relying on a single number for overall production rates when he provides an alternative to a competitiveness approach. To say that 91 percent of the slowdown in the growth of per capita GNP "was explained by a decline in domestic productivity growth" does not explain the decline but rephrases it. To say that GNP grew slowly because the growth in output per hour grew slowly is simply to push aside the real question: What caused the decline? Krugman's numerical exercise does not even adequately fulfill the smaller role he assigns to it—to show that foreign competition played a trivial part in lowering the rate of growth of national welfare. This failure occurs because Krugman counts only the prices and quantities of imports, not their impact on profits, investment, jobs and wages. The typical case outlining the advantages of trade to the U.S. economy always focuses on these elements because they are much bigger than the simple, first-round effects of the prices and quantities of imports, which, with a modicum of craftsmanship, can be manipulated to demonstrate whatever one wishes. Similar problems of logic and data flaw the calculations that yield Krugman's most sweeping single-number assertion—that the U.S. trade deficit in manufactured goods has only a very small impact on wages, a reduction at most of only 0.3 percent. The problem, again, is not just with the single number but with the static approach Krugman adopts. Only a dynamic understanding and methodology can appreciate those impacts because that is how they proceed, iteratively, with real and consequential feedback. Finally, national productivity data have several smaller, technical difficulties that radically reduce the reliability of the numbers. It is impossible to get reliable productivity numbers for the core sectors of the service economy, for example—well over a third of GNP. And operationally, market and institutional structures lead economists to assign low productivity growth rates to industries such as semiconductors although engineers know that productivity has grown at fabulous rates.

The clean simplicity and apparent analytic power of the simple, one-number approach, though it fits snugly with the models and methods of traditional American economics, has given rise to efforts to define a different organizing concept—competitiveness—in order to open a broader, more open-minded and modest approach. The competitiveness approach poses a sensible question: How are we doing as an economy? No single number sums it all up, especially given the follow-up: How are we doing compared to the other guys? And why? Competitiveness is a reconsideration of a broad set of indicators, none of which tells the whole story but that together provide a highly legitimate focus.

STEPHEN S. COHEN
Professor and Co-Director of the Berkeley Roundtable on the International Economy, University of California, Berkeley. An expanded version of this response will be published by BRIE in July 1994.

Careless Arithmetic

BENN STEIL

Paul Krugman has done everyone a service in warning against the dangers of making policy on the basis of facile analogies, such as those between countries and corporations. Yet while he

justifiably accuses others of "careless arithmetic" in making their case, he shows little concern with immunizing himself from the charge. With regard to European labor costs, he cites Sam Brittan (*Financial Times,* June 1, 1993) in asserting that they "have not risen in relative terms when the exchange rate adjustment is made." Thus he concludes that European firms have not suffered a decline in competitiveness, as British Prime Minister John Major had claimed. In fact, Brittan's statistics show that between 1987 and 1993 European Community unit labor costs in manufacturing rose approximately 19 percent as compared with only 5 percent in the United States, both before and after the exchange rate adjustment. How Krugman could have missed this point, as he put it, "cries out for an explanation."

BENN STEIL
Senior Research Fellow for the International Economics Programme, The Royal Institute of International Affairs

Response

Proving My Point

Paul Krugman

My article in the March/April issue of *Foreign Affairs* has obviously upset many people. Some of my critics claim that I misrepresented their position, that despite their insistent use of the word "competitiveness" they have never believed that the major industrial nations are engaged in a competitive economic struggle. Others claim that I have gotten the economics wrong: that countries *are* engaged in a competitive struggle. Indeed, some of them make both claims in the same response.

MOVING TARGET

Lester C. Thurow vigorously denies ever asserting that international competition is a central issue for the U.S. economy. In particular, he cites page counts from his 1985 book, *The Zero-Sum Solution*, to demonstrate that domestic factors are his principal concern. But Thurow's most recent book is *Head to Head*, which follows its provocative title with the subtitle, *The Coming Battle Among Japan, Europe and America*. The book jacket asserts that the "decisive war of the century has

begun." The text asserts over and over that the major economic powers are now engaged in "win-lose" competition for world markets, a competition that has taken the place of the military competition between East and West. Thurow now says that international strategic competition is no more than seven percent of the problem; did the typical reader of *Head to Head* get this message?

Similarly, Stephen S. Cohen denies that he, or indeed anyone else with whom I should "deign to take difference," has ever said the things I claim competitiveness advocates believe. But in 1987 Cohen, together with John Zysman, published *Manufacturing Matters*, a book that seemed to say two (untrue) things: the long-term downward trend in the share of manufacturing in U.S. employment is largely due to foreign competition, and this declining share is a major economic problem.

After their initial denial, both Cohen and Thurow proceed to argue that international competition is of crucial importance after all. In this they are joined by

---

PAUL KRUGMAN is Professor of Economics at the Massachusetts Institute of Technology.

Clyde V. Prestowitz, Jr., who at least makes no bones about believing that trade and trade policy are the central issue for the U.S. economy. Does Cohen believe that Prestowitz—or James Fallows, who expressed similar views in his new book, *Looking at the Sun*—is one of those people with whom I should not deign to argue?

SLOPPY MATH: PART II

Of all the elements in my article, the section on careless arithmetic—the strange pattern of errors in reporting or using data in articles and books on competitiveness—has enraged the most people. Both Thurow and Prestowitz have taken care to fill their responses with a blizzard of numbers and calculations. However, some of the numbers are puzzling.

For example, Thurow says that imports are 14 percent of U.S. GDP, while exports are only 10 percent, and that reducing imports to equal exports would add $250 billion to the sales of U.S. manufacturers. But according to *Economic Indicators*, the monthly statistical publication of the Joint Economic Committee, U.S. imports in 1993 were only 11.4 percent of GDP, while exports were 10.4 percent. Even the current account deficit, a broader measure that includes some additional debit items, was only $109 billion. If the United States were to cut imports by $250 billion, far from merely balancing its trade as Thurow asserts, the United States would run a current account *surplus* of $140 billion—that is,

more than the 2 percent maximum of GDP U.S. negotiators have demanded Japan set as a target!

Or consider Prestowitz, who derides my claim that high-technology industries, commonly described as "high value" sectors, actually have much lower value added per worker than traditional "high volume," heavy industrial sectors. I have aggregated too much by looking at broad sectors like electronics, he says; I should look at the highest-tech lines of business, like semiconductors, where value added per worker is $234,000. Prestowitz should report the results of his research to the Department of Commerce, whose staff has obviously incorrectly calculated (in the *Annual Survey of Manufactures*) that in 1989 value added per worker in Standard Industrial Classification 3674 (semiconductors and related devices) was $96,487—closer to the $76,709 per worker in SIC 2096 (potato chips and related snacks) than to the $187,569 in SIC 3711 (motor vehicles and car bodies).[1]

Everyone makes mistakes, although it is surprising when men who are supposed to be experts on international competition do not have even a rough idea of the size of the U.S. trade deficit or know how to look up a standard industrial statistic. The interesting point, however, is that the mistakes made by Thurow, Prestowitz and other competitiveness advocates are not random errors; they are always biased in the same direction. That is, the advocates always err in a direction that makes

---

[1] I don't know why Thurow thinks the U.S. trade deficit is four times as big as it actually is. I have, however, tracked down Prestowitz's number. It is not value added per employee; it is shipments (which are always larger than value added) divided by the number of production workers (who are only a fraction of total employment, especially in high-technology industries).

international competition seem more important than it really is.

Beyond these petty, if revealing, errors of fact are a series of conceptual misunderstandings. For example, Prestowitz argues that productivity in sectors that compete on world markets is much more important than productivity in non-traded service sectors because the former

Friedrich List, the new cult figure

determine wage rates throughout the economy. For example, because U.S. manufacturing workers are much more productive than their Third World counterparts, U.S. barbers, who do not have a comparable productivity advantage, also get high wages. But Prestowitz fails to notice that the converse is also true: service productivity affects the real wages of manufacturing workers. Because the high relative productivity of U.S. manufacturing is not matched in the haircut sector, haircuts by those well-paid barbers are much more expensive than haircuts in the Third World; as a result real wages of U.S. manufacturing workers (that is, wages in terms of what they can buy, including haircuts) are not as high as they would be if U.S. barbers were more productive. With careful thought, one realizes that real wages depend on the overall productivity of the economy, with no special presumption that productivity in

manufacturing—or in internationally traded sectors in general—deserves any more attention or active promotion than productivity elsewhere.

Cohen makes essentially the same mistake when he complains that I underestimated the effects of competitive pressure because I focused only on import and export prices and did not consider the further impacts of that pressure on profits and wages. He somehow fails to realize that a change in wages or profits that is not reflected in import or export prices cannot change overall U.S. real income—it can only redistribute profits to one group within the United States at the expense of another. That is why the effect of international price competition on U.S. real income can be measured by the change in the ratio of export to import prices—full stop. And the effects of changes in this ratio on the U.S. economy have, as I showed in my article, been small.

Or consider Thurow's analysis of the benefits that would accrue to the United States if it could roll back imports (leaving aside the inaccuracy of his numbers). He asserts that the United States could create five million new jobs in import-competing sectors, and he assumes that all five million jobs represent a net addition to employment. But this assumption is unrealistic. As this reply was being written, the Federal Reserve was raising interest rates in an effort to rein in a recovery that it feared would proceed too far, that is, lead to excessive employment, producing a renewed surge in inflation. Some people think that the Fed is tightening too soon, but the essential point is that the growth of employment is not determined by the ability of the United States to sell goods on world markets or to compete with imports, but by the Fed's judgement of what will not set off inflation. So suppose that the United States were to impose import quotas, adding millions of jobs in import-competing sectors. The Fed would respond by raising interest rates to prevent an overheated economy, and most if not all of the job gains would be matched by job losses elsewhere.

THINGS ADD UP

In each of these cases, my critics seem to have forgotten the most basic principle of economics: things add up. Higher employment in import-competing industries must come either through a reduction in unemployment, in which case one must ask whether the implied unemployment rate (about three percent in Thurow's example) is feasible, or at the expense of jobs elsewhere in the economy, in which case no overall job gain takes place. If higher manufacturing wages lead to a higher wage rate for barbers without higher tonsorial productivity, the gain must come at someone else's expense. Since it is hard to see how foreigners pay for more expensive American haircuts, that wage gain can only redistribute the

benefits of manufacturing productivity from one set of American workers to another, not increase the total gains. In their haste to assign great importance to international competition, my critics, like the inventors of perpetual motion machines, have failed to realize that there are conservation principles that any story about the economy must honor.

But perhaps Cohen, Thurow and Prestowitz stumble on economic basics because they are so eager to get to their main point, which is that advanced economic theory, and in particular the theory of strategic trade policy, supports their obsession with competitiveness.

Prestowitz's central assertion is that the theory of strategic trade policy, which he for some reason thinks I invented in a paper about aircraft competition (the actual inventors were James Brander and Barbara Spencer, who never mentioned aircraft), justifies aggressively interventionist trade policies. He further asserts that economists in general, and I in particular, have run away from that implication for ideological reasons.

Well, that's not quite the real story. It is true that in the early 1980s professional economists became aware that one of the implications of new theories of international trade was a possible role for strategic policies to promote exports in certain industries. Confronted with a new idea that was exciting, potentially important but untested, these economists began a sustained process of research, probing the weak points, confronting the new idea with the data. After all, lots of things could be true in principle. For example in certain theoretical situations a tax cut could definitely stimulate the economy so much that government revenues would actually rise, and it would be very nice if that were the actual situation; but unfortunately it isn't. Similarly, it is definitely possible to imagine a situation in which, because of all of the market imperfections Thurow dwells on, a clever strategic trade policy would sharply raise U.S. real income. And it would be very nice if the United States could devise such a policy. But is that possibility really there? To answer that question requires looking hard at the facts.

And so over the course of the last ten years a massive international research program has explored the prospects for strategic trade policy.[2] Two broad conclusions emerge. First, to identify which industries should receive strategic promotion or the appropriate form and level of promotion is very difficult. Second, the payoffs of even a successful strategic trade policy are likely to be very modest—certainly far less even than Thurow's "seven percent solution," which is closer to the entire share of international trade in the U.S. economy.

Research results are always open to challenge, especially in an inexact field like economics. If Prestowitz wants to point out specific failings in the dozens of painstaking empirical studies of strategic trade that have been carried out over the past decade, by all means let him do so. His remarks about the subject, however, strongly suggest that while he is happy to mention strategic trade theory in support of his policy writing, Prestowitz has not read any of the economic literature.

I do, however, agree with Prestowitz on one point. More people should read the works of Friedrich List. If they do, they may wonder why this turgid, confused writer—whose theory led him to predict that Holland and Denmark would be condemned to permanent economic backwardness unless they sought political union with Germany—has suddenly become a favorite of Fallows, Prestowitz and others. The new cult of List bears an uncanny resemblance to the right-wing supply-siders' canonization of the classical French economist Jean-Baptiste Say, who claimed that the economy as a whole could never suffer from the falls in aggregate demand that produce recessions.[3] The motive of the supply-siders was, of course, to cover simplistic ideas with a veneer of faux scholarship.

In contrast to Prestowitz and Thurow, who offer coherent if flawed reasons to worry about international competition,

---

[2] The original paper on strategic trade policy was James Brander and Barbara Spencer, "Export Subsidies and International Market Share Rivalry," *Journal of International Economics*, February 1985, pp. 83-100. See also Paul Krugman, ed., *Strategic Trade Policy and the New International Economics*, Cambridge: MIT Press, 1986; Robert Feenstra, ed., *Empirical Methods for International Trade*, Chicago: University of Chicago Press, 1988; Robert Baldwin, ed., *Trade Policy Issues and Empirical Analysis*, Chicago: University of Chicago Press, 1988; and Paul Krugman and Alasdair Smith, eds., *Empirical Studies of Strategic Trade Policy*, Chicago: University of Chicago Press, 1994.

[3] Fallows officially elevated List to guru status in his article "How the World Works," *The Atlantic Monthly*, December 1993, pp. 60-87. Readers may wish to compare the elevation of Say by Jude Wanniski in his influential supply-side tract, *The Way the World Works*, New York: Basic Books, 1978.

Cohen offers a more difficult target. Basically, he asks us to accept "competitiveness" as a kind of ineffable essence that cannot be either defined or measured. Data that seem to suggest the importance of this essence are cited as "indicators," whatever that means, while those that do not are dismissed as unreliable. Both in his article and other writings he has persistently used a rhetoric that seems to portray international trade as a game with winners and losers, but when challenged on any particular point he denies having said it. I guess I don't understand how a concept so elusive can be a useful guide to policy.

My original article in *Foreign Affairs* argued that a doctrine that views world trade as a competitive struggle has become widely accepted, that this view is wrong but that there is nonetheless an intense desire to believe in that doctrine. The article enraged many, especially when it asserted that the desire to believe in competitive struggle repeatedly leads highly intelligent authors into surprising lapses in their handling of concepts and data. I could not, however, have asked for a better demonstration of my point than the responses published in this issue. ☯

Why Pressure Tokyo?

Roger C. Altman

The strained relations between Japan and the United States cannot be explained by spurious charges that the Clinton administration is pushing managed trade, capitalizing on anti-Japanese sentiment to score domestic political points or needlessly bashing Japan over economically meaningless international surpluses. Rather, the tensions arise from two fundamental and related developments: changed American priorities and the pronounced drag of Japan's huge current account surplus on global demand, economic expansion and job creation.

The Clinton administration's drive to spur global economic growth and strengthen U.S. economic potential requires a new deal with Japan. For itself and all other nations, the United States is seeking to converge Japan's international accounts with the rest of the industrialized world and to open Japan's markets.

NO MORE FREE RIDE

The search for such convergence marks a transition in U.S.-Japan relations—the fourth such transition since World War II. First came the reconstruction period, running through the early 1950s, in which the United States consciously helped rebuild Japan's industrial capacity in order to make democracy permanent. The United States tolerated Japan's protection of home markets, its resurrection of certain prewar practices and the resulting *keiretsu* structure of industrial cross-share holdings, in which companies cooperate informally.

The second phase began with the 1952 Mutual Security Assistance Pact, which ended U.S. occupation of Japan. The pact extended the U.S. nuclear umbrella over Japan and made Japan the Asian cornerstone of the Cold War containment strategy. Japan became vital to the defense of Pacific sea-lanes and host to the largest U.S. military base in the region. Although economic issues were steadily emerging, they remained secondary to security interests.

Japan's growing economic prowess

ROGER C. ALTMAN is Deputy Secretary of the Treasury for the Clinton administration.

ushered in the third phase, which lasted from the early 1970s until the end of the Cold War. During that period economic policy differences and trade frictions continually rose even while the security issue remained paramount. Japanese firms, assisted by Tokyo's administrative guidance and targeted industrial policies, became world-class producers and successful competitors for export markets. Aided by massive domestic savings and an undervalued yen, Japan ran growing trade and current account surpluses with the rest of the world, especially the United States. U.S. pressure on Japan to open its home market produced a pattern whereby the Japanese government engaged in protracted trade negotiations while opening its economy as little as possible. When agreements were finally reached, they were often vaguely worded and subject to conflicting interpretations.

Beginning in 1993, the U.S.-Japan relationship was jolted into its fourth phase by newly elected President Clinton, whose sense of post-Cold War priorities put economic matters first. Assessing the relationship, his administration found the security component to be solid and cooperation on global development and environmental issues to be in working order. But the economic dimension was badly in need of repair and required a new perspective on Japan. A diminished need for a bulwark against Soviet expansionism accompanied a rise of other viable economic partners in the Asia-Pacific region. Within the United States, public attention sharply shifted toward unmet domestic needs. The electorate wanted a leader whose primary focus was jobs and economic growth at home. And in trade competition, the public, business and Congress clamored for tough action to level the playing fields, particularly with Japan.

MEASURABLE RESULTS

The Clinton administration conceived its policy on three broad premises. The first premise was that ending stagnation at home required key initiatives, of which the first was congressional passage of the president's $500 billion deficit reduction plan. The second premise was that Japan's trade surplus of $130 billion ($50 billion with the United States) was too large to be sustained. Weak stimulus packages were inadequately addressing this surplus, despite Japan's structural budget surplus. The third premise was that continued recalcitrance explained why Japan's imports of manufactured goods represented only 3.1 percent of Japan's GNP compared to an average of 7.4 percent for other Group of Seven countries. Further out of line, Japan's incoming foreign direct investment stood at 0.7 percent of GDP versus 28.6 percent for the United States and 38.5 percent for Europe.

Japan's import and investment penetration problem reflects a series of longstanding visible and invisible trade barriers that have proved impervious to sectoral negotiations, structural impediment initiatives and investment access agreements. Thus a fresh U.S. approach was needed. The new relationship required a framework encompassing both macroeconomic and trade policy. Stronger domestic demand-led growth in Japan would help facilitate import penetration. The trade component would focus on removing structural and sectoral barriers to raise the quantity of imports the Japanese will buy when their incomes increase and thereby reduce the current account imbalance. After tough negotiating, the framework agreement of July 1993 committed both parties to four basic commitments, two on each side.

The Clinton administration committed to further deficit reduction efforts and policies to raise savings and improve competitiveness. The administration also pledged a continued openness of U.S. domestic markets provided that Japan holds up its end of the bargain.

For its part, Japan agreed to pursue policies that over the "medium term" would lead to a "highly significant" reduction in its global current account surpluses. The United States made clear that it interpreted "highly significant" to mean a fall in those surpluses from 3.5 percent of GDP to below 2 percent. Further, the United States defined the "medium term" to mean three to four years. Japan's second commitment was to pursue structural and sectoral policies that would lead to a significant increase in imports from all countries (not just the United States) over the same period. The American interpretation of "significant" was a one-third increase. In fairness, however, the U.S. interpretation in both cases was unilateral. Japan fiercely resisted quantifying these areas in the agreement and acknowledges only that the United States has such interpretations.

Nevertheless, in a significant departure from past agreements, a provision called for "qualitative or quantitative indicators" to measure progress. To the United States, this provision meant the two countries had finally agreed to a dialogue

on measurable results. But the ink had barely dried on this provision before a fierce public relations campaign ensued against the use of such indicators. The Japanese claimed the agreement represented managed trade and that such a results-oriented approach is antithetical to liberalized trade. Indeed, they argued, the United States was demanding market-share targets in key sectors similar to those granted in the now-infamous 1986 semiconductor agreement.

The rhetorical campaign has been skillful, and many editorialists and economists have joined the criticism. To be fair, the Clinton administration has occasionally compounded the problem by sending ambiguous signals. But Japan's rhetorical campaign does not withstand close scrutiny. The Japanese government that berates the United States on charges of managed trade has long been in the business of targeting market outcomes itself. Furthermore the same government agencies that make these pronouncements have tolerated a remarkable degree of collusion among private Japanese companies at the expense of foreign firms.

The reality is that the agreement does not mandate market-share targets, and the United States is not seeking targets. The issues are goals and measurability. In any particular sector, the U.S. aim is to negotiate a series of long-term goals and objective standards against which progress can be judged. The overall goal should be convergence toward international standards of market openness. Moreover, any particular sector can have several measurements. In the auto sector, for example, measurements might include increases in Japanese dealerships that sell both foreign and Japanese cars and domestic content levels in Japanese cars produced in the United States. The framework would measure progress against a series of these indicators of which no one measure would dominate.

The goal of market openness cannot be seriously disputed. It can be achieved almost entirely by deregulation, and that had been a central theme of Japanese Prime Minister Morihiro Hosokawa. And measurable results have no good argument to oppose them. If fair measures are chosen, the entire world can judge whether progress has occurred or not. Nor is the framework an attempt to reconstruct Japan in the U.S. image. The U.S. emphasis on results is precisely designed to shift the debate away from changing the nature of the Japanese economic system.

This new approach is not a bilateral deal for the United States and Japan. The U.S. goal is to open Japanese markets for the benefit of producers from all countries; reducing trade barriers is sought solely on a most-favored-nation basis. The new framework is not only consistent with the principles of the General Agreement on Tariffs and Trade, but, insofar as Japan's closed markets and unbalanced trade represent a major threat to the soundness of the multilateral trading system, the framework is essential to the viability of the GATT system.

The framework is also essential to maintaining support for further market-opening agreements around the world. For example, congressional support for the North American Free Trade Agreement or GATT cannot be obtained if Japan's import penetration problem is simply accepted. Those who say that the growth and job gains from opening Japanese markets are trivial and that the whole effort is misguided show no appreciation for this reality. In Washington, it is a matter of fairness.

The framework's objectives are consistent with the basic aspirations of people everywhere: lower prices, greater consumer choice and higher living standards, a reduction in international tensions and an improvement in their nation's standing. These principles have particular resonance today, given the new Japanese government's emphasis on improving the lot of the Japanese consumer.

IT'S JAPAN'S MOVE

Unfortunately, the two sides were unable to meet the framework's first six-month deadline for sub-agreements in the procurement, automotive and insurance sectors. Moreover, the macroeconomic developments were also disappointing. Tokyo announced a six trillion yen tax cut, ostensibly to boost domestic demand and work down the current account surplus. But the cut took the form of a rebate, with no assurance of lasting after one year. Such one-time tax cuts usually induce savings rather than spending and do not provide meaningful stimulus. Indeed, most analysts estimated that the tax cut would add only 0.7 percent to growth in 1994 and would cut the current account surplus by only $2 billion. The United States registered its disappointment with the tax package.

President Clinton and Prime Minister Hosokawa acknowledged these failures during their remarkably candid summit on February 11. The president noted a particular disagreement over the issue of targets. He reaffirmed that the United States was not seeking guaranteed market outcomes, which is how most observers interpret the term "targets." He noted, however, that Japan feared that any goals would ultimately be interpreted as mandatory targets. As a result, therefore, Tokyo was unwilling to accept a combination of goals and measurements. For its part, Washington was adamant. "No agreement was better than an empty agreement," the president said.

Now the talks are suspended and both sides agree that the ball is in Japan's court. Discussions will only recommence if Tokyo develops a new proposal that responds to the framework criteria. After a cooling-off period, there is no reason why such an initiative should not come forward.

In the interim, the United States is taking some unilateral steps. The first has been to reexamine existing trade disputes and seek negotiated solutions or apply sanctions. An obvious example of this step was the cellular phone case and the finding that Japan was in violation. Almost all neutral observers agreed that Motorola had been denied a fair market opportunity. That is why Japan moved and a good agreement ensued, as had happened a few months earlier in the construction case. The second step involved the reimposition by executive order of the Super 301 trade tool. This tool requires identifying, every six months, "priority practices in priority countries" that violate Section 301 of the U.S. trade law. No such countries or practices will be designated before September 30. The administration carefully chose a flexible version of this tool, not the heavy-handed approach favored by some in Congress.

Other steps will be taken in a calm, deliberate manner. This is not a trade war, nor will it spin out of control. The United States will move only where the substance of a dispute is clear. Ultimately, the U.S.-Japan relationship will surmount this period of friction. These are the two largest economies in the world and they are highly interdependent. The security relationship remains strong and important, and the two nations share a vital agenda on global political cooperation.

The time has come for Japan to move toward global convergence in terms of its international accounts and the openness of its markets. On these points, industrialized nations concur even if some disagree with the particulars of the American approach. What issues and challenges will dominate the next century are unclear, but two things are certain: economics will be at the center of international affairs, and the U.S.-Japan partnership will play a key role in determining the course of global events. The Clinton administration is committed to charting a new course of relations with Japan that builds on these emerging realities.✪

Samurais No More

Jagdish Bhagwati

The failure of the February 11 Hosokawa-Clinton summit in Washington to produce a trade agreement on U.S. terms was marked by theatrics on the American side. Deputy Treasury Secretary Roger Altman's banter was typical. He declared, with the bluntness that Wall Street breeds, that the United States would wait "until hell freezes over" for the Japanese to accept U.S. demands. When Prime Minister Hosokawa finally said no to them, the American anger was palpable.

U.S. Trade Representative Mickey Kantor brought to center stage the Motorola cellular phones dispute, which the administration had readied to coincide with the summit by speeding up ongoing negotiations. Amenable to manipulation as "proof" of Japan's perfidy, the dispute was also the one most likely to be settled at a low cost, financial and political, by the Hosokawa government to save U.S. face: a crumb thrown to the United States, it could be called a cake.

Indeed Japan ended the dispute by bribing Motorola with investment outlays while affirming the dispute's uniqueness and reiterating the policy of saying no. The Clinton administration, predictably, performed a war dance, celebrating a victory in a skirmish as if it had won the war, attributing the Motorola settlement to American resolve and threats, particularly to the president's revival in March of the "Super 301" weapon, which authorizes the administration to highlight countries it determines are trading unfairly and, if it chooses, to impose trade sanctions in retaliation.

BREAKING ITS OWN RULES

The Clinton administration, however, cannot conceal the reality that its policy is fatally flawed. The policy makes demands that are inconsistent with the

JAGDISH BHAGWATI is Arthur Lehman Professor of Economics at Columbia University and was the Economic Policy Advisor to the Director-General of the General Agreement on Tariffs and Trade. He is completing, with Gary Saxonhouse, *The Jaundiced Eye: Perceptions of Japan in the World Economy.*

very principles on which the United States has itself provided leadership in shaping the world trading system over half a century. As important, the policy fails to grasp the significant changes that make both the style and the substance of these demands unacceptable to the new Japan. American policy is thus both unworthy and unworkable.

The problems with that policy concern "quantities" and "process." The United States wants managed trade: specifically, it wants the Japanese government to accept numerical benchmarks and targets for increased imports in specific sectors. It is also pressing for one-way concessions from Japan in areas where the United States has judged Japan to be either closed to imports or in violation of treaty obligations, acting unilaterally instead of using impartial procedures to which Japan would also have recourse. In both respects, the United States has the double disadvantage of having been roundly condemned by other nations and of having not the remotest chance of acceptance by Japan.

Benchmarks are only a weasel word for targets (that is, quotas), and these import targets quickly turn into export protectionism: they work to guarantee for American firms a share of the foreign market just as conventional import protectionism gives firms a guaranteed share of the domestic market.

These targets will multiply because they are open to manipulation by domestic firms that seek assured export markets. When Japan unwisely accepted the Reagan administration's demand for a numerical benchmark (for the first time in U.S.-Japan trade negotiations), economists had forecast that other firms and industries would soon jump on the bandwagon. It was too rewarding a precedent not to exploit, and indeed that is exactly what has happened. Now a complaisant administration has become the agent for the lobbyists of industries such as autos, auto parts and medical equipment, seeking to impose many more such agreements on Japan.

The proliferation of such import targets to several sectors would also bring other countries onto the scene demanding their own guaranteed share of the Japanese market. The reason is plain enough: Japan must be fully aware that if it opens up to imports but those imports do not come from the United States, the pressure from Washington will continue. So Japan will have a powerful incentive to divert its imports from other nations to the United States, even if the United States pretends that its objective is to open the Japanese economy, not throw contracts the way of American firms. Hence, properly fearing trade diversion, the European Union has always said that if Japan concedes import targets to the United States, the EU will be right behind.

If numbers rather than rules are accepted as the way to conduct trade, the prospect is then certain that Japanese industry would soon be subject to heavy regulation and compelled to produce the politically agreed market shares. This would be bad enough for Japan. But it would also be a low blow to the rules-based world trading system that the United States has professed to uphold at the General Agreement on Tariffs and Trade.

In consequence, the United States, traditionally the leader on trade issues to the applause of economists, has found itself opposed by economists, whether Democrats or Republicans. There is also little support for America's Super 301-aided unilateralism. Washington is isolated when it wants to take the law in its own hands, especially now that the Uruguay Round has produced a binding settlement procedure. Even if Japan were guilty as charged, it is unacceptable that the United States should become complainant, judge and jury.

THE NEW JAPAN

Japan's resistance to U.S. demands was urged worldwide—from Europe in particular—undoubtedly strengthening Hosokawa's resolve to say no. But that resolve comes from within Japan itself, reflecting the nuanced yet remarkable changes that Japan is undergoing. The Clinton administration simply does not get it: the new Japan is trying to be like the old United States just as the new United States, with its flirtation with industrial policy, embrace of demands for managed trade, and (as in the president's announcement of the Saudi purchase of U.S. aircraft) unabashed use of political muscle rather than economic competitiveness to succeed in world markets, is trying to be like the old Japan.

Hosokawa, and the large numbers of reform-minded Japanese who voted the Liberal Democratic Party out of power, wish an end to old-fashioned regulation. Managed trade would turn the clock back when they want to push it forward. The reformers also believe in reciprocal rights and obligations; they reject unilateralism and want multilateralism; they want due process, not the peremptory judgments of the United States (which reflect the self-serving finger-pointing of individual U.S. companies).

Ironically, but predictably, these are American ideas. They have spread rapidly to Japan because, among other reasons, Japan has large numbers of its young citizens abroad. Over 40,000 Japanese students are in the United States today, learning to put their feet on the table in the classroom instead of meekly bowing to the *sensei* (the venerable teacher). With the dramatic shift in the 1980s in the share of Japanese direct foreign investment away from the poor countries to the rich, prompted in part by the outbreak of protectionism in the EU and in the United States, which restricted export access to these markets, great numbers of Japanese women and children also live in the West. They are a subversive, modernizing force. Increased numbers of Japanese academics can now be found on U.S. campuses, speaking English fluently and working with Americans at the frontiers of science when only a decade ago there were practically none.

The Japan that was so set on what the historian Henry Smith has aptly called "controlled openness"—drawing carefully on what it liked in other cultures rather than abandoning itself, like the United States, to free cultural influx and experimentation—is now beyond such control. The globalization of the Japanese economy and modern communications imposes its own logic on the nation. But the Clinton aides in charge of Japan policy, mainly Wall Street luminaries and high-profile lawyer-lobbyists with lifestyles that leave little room for reflection and put a premium on going for the jugular, appear to be ignorant of this historic transformation. These Clinton warriors think they are fighting the samurai when they are facing GIs.

Indeed, these aides manifested their lack of comprehension of the new Japan with tactical errors in negotiations leading up to the summit. The bureaucrats in Japan were assumed to be the problem. The new politicians, keen on reform, were assumed to be U.S. allies in seeing the manifest virtue of demands for managed trade to "open Japan." But the new politicians were the ones who had principled objections to managed trade and also to U.S. unilateralism.

While the United States was pretending that benchmarks were different from targets, Kantor did not even bother to dissimulate when, in the semiconductor agreement, the U.S. market share fell recently below the 20 percent benchmark; instead he came out swinging with both hands, complaining about the shortfall as if the benchmark were a target and demanding corrective action. Moreover, the president, indulging in Japan-bashing to promote the North American Free Trade Agreement, had already promised revival of Super 301, taking the incentive away from the Japanese to settle on U.S. terms in order to avoid the provision's reenactment. The Clinton aides failed to understand that their twin assumptions about Japan—that nothing but bluster can succeed and that bluster cannot fail— were no longer valid.

In the end, the flaw in U.S. policy derives from the exaggeration of Japan's differences of yesterday as much as from an ignorance of its rapid convergence to the United States today. Washington is obsessed with the view that Japan is different and special, a predatory exporter and an exclusionary importer that must be dealt with as an outlaw, what Jonathan Rauch has called an "outnation," with tough external *gaiatsu* (foreign pressure) and targets to restrain exports and expand imports.

Economic analysis hardly supports such stereotypes. The simpleminded assertion coming from the Clinton administration that, because Japan's share of manufactured imports in GNP is below the average of the Group of Seven industrialized nations, Japan "underimports" and has a closed market requiring special measures is nonsense. By that token, since Canada's share is substantially higher than the United States', the United States should be judged closed relative to Canada. Sophisticated econometric studies of the question are badly divided; the better-crafted of these certainly do not support the thesis that Japan imports too little, nor do they indicate a special and extraordinary effect of informal trade barriers that make Japan a fit case for unusual treatment in the world trading system.

Even the imports by Japan of manufactured goods, a persistent source of complaint, have grown in the last decade to over half of its imports. Moreover, the foreign share in many of Japan's high-tech markets, so dear to Clintonites, is by no means static or small. The table on the following page, based on recently released data from the National Science Foundation, shows that in seven important high-tech markets, the U.S. and Japanese import shares look pretty similar, so much

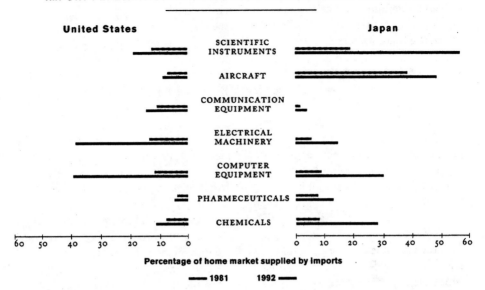

United States — Japan

SCIENTIFIC INSTRUMENTS
AIRCRAFT
COMMUNICATION EQUIPMENT
ELECTRICAL MACHINERY
COMPUTER EQUIPMENT
PHARMECEUTICALS
CHEMICALS

60 50 40 30 20 10 0   0 10 20 30 40 50 60

Percentage of home market supplied by imports

—— 1981   1992 ——

so that if the industries and the countries were blacked out, one could well mistake the U.S. chart for Japan's.

The notion of Japan's overwhelming difference nonetheless persists because it is reinforced by the egregious fallacy, often repeated by the president and his aides in public, that Japan's huge bilateral surplus with the United States is surefire proof that Japan's markets are closed, requiring a concentration of one's wrath and energy on Japan. Occasionally, counterintuitive economic sense will prevail for a moment, but then fallacy, so compelling to the untrained mind, resurfaces. Convincing Washington that bilateral surpluses are no index of the openness of markets is as difficult as convincing a peasant that the earth is round when it appears flat to his naked eye.

Nor does Japan's multilateral surplus set it apart as wicked and bizarre. Its per-

sistence is shorter-lived than America's own surplus in the two decades after the Second World War. Japan's surplus reflects its excess of domestic savings over investment and is generally to be applauded as a contribution to world net savings at a time of huge demand for investible funds in the developing and the former socialist countries. In the immediate short run, Japan can certainly contribute to its own recovery and indirectly help the United States by undertaking the significant fiscal stimulus that Hosokawa had worked to get. But all macroeconomists agree that the spillover or "locomotive" effect of Japanese stimulus on U.S. prosperity will be small, making even this obsession of the Clinton administration seem strange. In short, nothing here requires that the United States think that Japan is "off the curve" in responsible macroeconomic management: its mistakes are no more gargantuan than those of the United States, for example, during the decade of fiscal irresponsibility from which it has just emerged.

COOPERATION, NOT CONFRONTATION

The cancer at the core of the U.S. policy then is the view that the United States needs a differential treatment of Japan and a special framework agreement. The justifications for that premise, never strong, are particularly implausible today. They must finally be abandoned.

There is nothing extraordinary even about the specific trade disputes with Japan. Similar complaints can be made with regard to other nations. The accounts of the delays experienced by Motorola in getting its cellular phone system adopted in the Tokyo-Nagoya corridor (one of two in Japan), for example, must be set against the facts that Motorola was not allowed to set up its own system at all in France and Germany and had to adapt to a different system there, and that entry into the U.S. market itself has been impeded by antidumping harassment. Such examples can be readily multiplied.

The time has come to admit that Japan must be allowed to trade by rules rather than quantities, and that the rules must include the adjudication of disputes by impartial procedures available to both parties. The notion that U.S.-Japan trade issues are so special that they must be dealt with bilaterally in a framework that permits the United States to impose one-way demands on Japan and to pronounce unilaterally its own verdicts that Japan has "failed to live up to its agreements" must finally be laid to rest.

Will the president, no stranger to principled and bold changes of course, rise to the occasion? It will not be easy: the failed trade policy toward Japan is most likely his own. After all, the North American Free Trade Agreement and the Uruguay Round were Republican initiatives; he needed one of his own. The Silicon Valley entrepreneurs were the first to swing to him during the campaign; he bought their view of Japan. He chose advisers that shared these jaundiced views. He chose a U.S. trade representative and a commerce secretary who proudly say that they disdain economic "theology" and want results; so they reflect interests, not principles, as they confront Japan.

The president may have fancied that he would have the glory of "opening Japan," as a sort of modern-day Commodore Perry. That historical parallel will not work. The tragedy is that, by persisting in the current policy, he may put two great nations on a course that may repeat history in less agreeable ways.

Beating Back Predatory Trade

Alan Tonelson

CONFOUNDING THE CONVENTIONAL WISDOM

CONTRARY TO WIDESPREAD beliefs, relief from predatory foreign trade practices has played a major role in revitalizing key American industries in recent years. Five major American industries—automotive, steel, machine tool, semiconductor and textile—have received significant relief from imports through intelligently structured trade laws. Those industries have confounded the predictions of laissez-faire economic ideologies by gaining market share at home and in some cases abroad, contributing to job creation and reinvigorating American competitiveness. Even in industries that have aggressively downsized since the early 1980s—such as the steel industry—relief from imports has prevented job loss from worsening. In addition, the cost of these programs is far smaller than commonly believed.

President Bill Clinton has given trade policy unprecedented attention not only by supporting the North American Free Trade Agreement (NAFTA) and the Uruguay Round of the General Agreement on Tariffs and Trade (GATT), but by making sallies against trade barriers in Europe and promoting American business in the Pacific Basin. Moreover, his efforts in the framework talks with Japan and recent export initiatives have sought to strengthen American industry and

ALAN TONELSON is Research Director of the Economic Strategy Institute. He wishes to acknowledge the research assistance of Nisha Mody and Hallet Hastert.

create high-wage jobs by opening foreign markets to U.S. goods. But the Clinton administration's policies and programs have come under attack from many foreign governments, who portray them as unilateral protectionism in violation of world trade law, and from many economists, who consider them threats to freer trade. On the contrary, if not addressed in the implementing legislation that must be passed by Congress, significant problems for the economy could be created by the recently signed Uruguay Round agreement. It could significantly dilute several U.S. trade laws and import relief programs, weakening America's ability to respond to predatory foreign trade practices.

THE IMPORT RELIEF RECORD

THE NOTION THAT import relief can achieve lasting net benefits clashes violently with the prevailing wisdom of laissez-faire economics. Protectionism of any kind or degree, many economists insist, only shelters inefficient companies and hinders the process of "creative destruction"—an oxymoron coined in 1942 by economist Joseph Schumpeter—the process through which capitalism unsettles people's lives through job losses and career changes but eventually enriches most of them.[1] In particular, this orthodoxy teaches that industries and companies receiving import relief grow lazy and greedy. Shielded from competition, these firms allegedly lose incentives to innovate, boost efficiency and hold down prices. Instead, they rest on their technological laurels, forget about quality, jack up prices and greedily suck windfall profits out of captive markets.

These textbook staples, however logical-sounding, have been completely contradicted by much of America's recent experience with

---

[1] Self-styled champions of free trade have largely succeeded in their efforts to attach fatally pejorative connotations to the terms "protection" and "protectionism"; thus, I opt for the term "import relief." But definitional considerations require its use as well. Free traders as a group, ironically, countenance numerous trade distortions, such as economic buffers for infant industries or defense manufacturers, but they regularly stigmatize advocates of import quotas, tariffs or enforcing U.S. trade laws as zealots who would create a hermetically sealed U.S. economy destined to implode. The mere term "protectionism" has become such a bugbear that it clouds debate and stifles fresh thinking on trade issues and national economic policy.

import relief. The U.S. automobile, semiconductor, machine tool, steel and textile industries all received significant import relief throughout the 1980s and 1990s. In all five industries—which total hundreds of companies, employ millions of workers and span the technological spectrum—new investments in plant, equipment and research and development surged, productivity shot up, quality improved and prices rose at rates very close to overall inflation rates, and sometimes below them. As documented in several studies, notably the Fall 1993 report by the McKinsey Global Institute, *Manufacturing Productivity*, Japan maintains a significant productivity lead in some of these industries. However, American manufacturers have not only improved their performance in absolute terms, but in some cases they have narrowed the gap. Most of the industries cited here recaptured market share from foreign competitors at home, abroad or both.

THE BIG THREE: BABY, YOU CAN DRIVE MY CAR

BATTERED BY fuel-efficient imports from Japan and a vicious cycle of poor management decisions, faltering productivity and deteriorating quality, the Big Three U.S. automakers—General Motors, Ford and Chrysler—secured import relief from the Reagan administration in 1981. Under pressure from Washington, Japan agreed to a so-called voluntary export restraint (VER) agreement that limited its exports of motor vehicles to the United States to 1.65 million units annually. The VER expired in 1987, but since then the Japanese have continued to stay well within its ceilings, in part because Japanese manufacturers shifted much assembly work to new U.S.-based transplant factories.

Detroit responded positively to the opportunity. By 1985, investment in new plant and equipment had reached a level double that of 1975 in real terms. And despite the explosion of technology-intensive information industries during the 1980s, the automobile industry slightly increased its share of total U.S. corporate research and development spending, to 12.4 percent. By 1984, the Big Three's productivity was rising at a 6.5 percent annual rate, compared with 3.3 percent for all U.S. manufacturing. For the entire 1980-1992 period, the industry's productivity increased by 44.2 percent. Meanwhile, U.S. vehicle and parts makers have pioneered development and commercialization of products, such as minivans and compact sport utility vehicles, as well as technologies, such as electronically controlled automatic transmissions, cab-forward design and integrated child seats.

Moreover, according to independent surveys, during the 1980s the Big Three significantly narrowed the gap with their Japanese competitors in many important areas, and in some cases overtook them. In 1980, for example, according to Consumers' Union, owners of Chrysler, Ford and General Motors vehicles reported 89, 100 and 109 defects per 100 cars in new model lines, respectively. The figures for Toyota, Honda and Nissan were 24, 34 and 47, respectively. By 1990, the Japanese figures had dropped to 14 for Honda, 15 for Nissan and 16 for Toyota. But the Chrysler, Ford and General Motors rates had plummeted to 31, 30 and 35, respectively. As of 1992, according to J.D. Power & Associates, six of the 14 best quality cars priced under $20,000—a range that is traditionally the strong suit of Japanese producers—were models of the Big Three.

> The Big Three have narrowed the gap with Japanese producers in many areas—and in some cases surpassed them.

In addition, despite the proliferation of Japanese transplant factories, Detroit is regaining a share of the U.S. motor vehicle market—posting nearly a full percentage point gain (to 73 percent) during 1993. And contrary to widespread charges of price gouging, the prices of American-made passenger cars increased less after the VER was imposed than before. From 1972 to 1980, car prices rose 62 percent—or 69 percent of the increase in the Consumer Price Index, less energy costs. In the eight years following the VER's imposition, car prices rose 32 percent, or 65 percent of the increase in the CPI, less energy costs. Since 1988, the rise in U.S. auto prices has been even slower—just 52 percent of the increase in the CPI. Despite the Big Three's comeback, however, the U.S. auto industry still faces a huge external problem: the closed automobile market in Japan. With the world's second-largest automobile market virtually impervious to imports, and with its producers consequently able to export from a sanctuary, a strong case for maintaining the VER can still be made.

STEELING MARKET SHARE

STARTING IN THE 1970s, the American steel industry went into a tailspin similar to that of the auto sector. The industry itself and unions were partly to blame. Investment in new technologies and facilities lagged while labor continually sought and received wage and benefit increases that far exceeded productivity gains. American steel makers faced structural problems as well. Because their Japanese and European competitors completely rebuilt their production bases after World War II (often with U.S. aid) they enjoyed state-of-the-art factories. As a result, America's share of world steel production fell from over 50 percent at the end of World War II to 26 percent in 1960 and 14.2 percent in 1980. In addition, many rich and poor countries alike saw steel as a road to riches and progress and thus heavily subsidized existing and new steel industries. Subsidies continued even after demand slumped in the 1970s, resulting in massive overcapacity.

Foreign steel sales rose from 12.4 percent of the U.S. market in 1973 to 18 percent in 1977 to a peak of 26.4 percent in 1984. Indeed, the United States has been the only major industrialized country to be a consistent net importer of steel in recent years. From 1977 to 1984, Washington instituted a series of "trigger price" arrangements designed to help U.S. steel-makers by preventing dumping by Japan and the European Community. But these measures failed, and in 1984 the Reagan administration was forced to attack the problem through a series of VERs and other bilateral trade agreements. These agreements, which did not go into effect until 1987, limited imports of finished steel to 18.5 percent of the U.S. market and imports of semifinished steel products to 20.2 percent of the market. In 1989 the Bush administration extended the VERs—with higher import limits—until March 1992, when they were allowed to expire. In 1989 the administration also began negotiating a multilateral steel agreement designed to end market-distorting steel trade practices, eliminate steel subsidies and open steel markets. A new round of multilateral steel talks began in June, but little progress has been made and little is expected in the near future.

Import relief gave the American steel industry a major opportunity to reinvent itself, and despite incurring operating losses of $7.4 billion during the 1980s, it seized the opportunity. Whereas the steel industry's capital expenditures fell from $2.6 billion in 1980 to $862 million in 1986, purchases of new plant and equipment bounced back to $2.5 billion by 1990. In fact, in fiscal 1991, the plant and equipment expenditures of the major U.S. steel companies far exceeded their cash flow. Moreover, much of the $22.5 billion invested by the industry in new plant and equipment from 1980 to 1989 was plainly due to the VER's stipulation that most of the industry's cash flow be plowed back into modernization and worker training.

The VERS had another important effect on new investment in the industry—they were largely responsible for attracting $3 billion of Japanese and Korean capital and cutting-edge production technology to American facilities, primarily for creating high-end products. The foreign resources poured into new ventures with U.S. partners and ensured that thousands of steel-making jobs stayed in the United States. With better factories and tools, American steel workers greatly boosted their productivity—by an average of 4.3 percent annually between 1980 and 1992. And the rates in America's cutting-edge minimills are even higher. In turn, heightened productivity and a cheaper dollar enabled U.S. companies—led by the minimills—to become among the world's lowest-cost steel producers. Indeed, the industry's costs per ton fell 20 percent between 1982 and 1992. Further, from 1982 to 1991, U.S. producer prices for the iron and steel sector rose only 14.1 percent, compared with a 16.5 percent figure for U.S. manufacturing industries as a whole. According to the industry's toughest judges—its customers—the quality of American steel products has steadily improved.

RETOOLING MACHINE TOOLS

TRADE RELIEF has helped the U.S. machine-tool industry bounce back as well. By 1986 the overvalued dollar, subsidized foreign competition and stiff trade barriers (including discriminatory procurement by foreign manufacturers operating in the United States) had helped foreign machine tool makers to grab an astounding 62 percent of the U.S. market. In the 1960s, the United States led the world in machine-tool production, with more than a fourth of international output; by 1986 its share had sunk below ten percent.

President Ronald Reagan recognized that the industry, which produces metal cutting and shaping devices, assembly machines, inspection and measuring machines, and automated manufacturing systems, was a "small but vital component of the U.S. industrial base." It represented an equally vital pillar of the defense industry. In 1986 the Reagan administration negotiated VERs with Japan and Taiwan on six classes of machine tools. The VERs were extended for two more years by President Bush in 1991 and finally expired at the end of 1993.

In the mid-1980s, dispirited by Washington's hands-off attitude, companies about to be affected by the VERs had begun disinvesting, with their ratio of capital spending to depreciation falling below 80 cents on the dollar. By 1992, seven years after the VERs were negotiated, the ratio had soared to $1.61 spent on new equipment for every dollar taken in depreciation. Research and development spending has jumped as well, from 5.2 percent of sales in 1987 to 11.9 percent in 1992. Moreover, VER-affected firms' prices rose only slightly during this period, and their pretax income remained well below that of U.S. manufacturers in general. In other words, far from pocketing profits, as laissez-faire theory predicts, machine tool makers receiving import relief put most of their earnings into improving their products. Machine-tool producer prices rose 34.6 percent between 1982 and 1991, but this increase was lower than the overall inflation rate of 37.9 percent.

> Machine-tool makers did not greedily pocket profits; earnings were put into improvements.

The results of this retooling have been a vast array of new products and dramatic progress in regaining old domestic markets and winning new foreign customers. From 1986 to 1992, machine-tool exports doubled, to $1 billion. In the world's fastest-growing machine-tool market, China, U.S. exports surged by 63 percent between 1987 and 1992. Japanese and German exports to China fell 30 percent and 12 percent, respectively, during those years. Meanwhile, on the home front, import penetration into the markets of VER-affected companies dropped from the 1986 peak of 62 percent to 49 percent in 1992.

SEMICONDUCTORS

SEMICONDUCTORS ARE the critical high-tech building blocks of American manufacturing, but in the mid-1980s this archetypal industry of the future faced a crisis as well. Illegal dumping, principally by Japanese producers, was driving U.S. semiconductor makers to the brink of bankruptcy. In both 1985 and 1986, the U.S. industry reported losses of nearly $2 billion, and 25,000 workers lost good jobs at good wages. U.S.-based chipmakers saw their share of world markets shrink from 57 percent in 1981 to 40 percent in 1987. During the same period, Japanese companies vaulted into first place, increasing their world market share from 33 percent to 48 percent.

In September 1986, the United States and Japan negotiated an agreement that the Reagan administration claimed committed Tokyo to boost foreign companies' share of the Japanese semiconductor market, the world's largest, to 20 percent within five years. The Japanese also unequivocally pledged to stop dumping. Yet dumping only stopped six months later, when Reagan imposed punitive tariffs on many Japanese electronics imports to protest Tokyo's continued obstinacy.

Rather than take the protection and run, the American semiconductor industry accelerated its retooling efforts. Research and development expenditures continued to increase at a whopping 17 percent annual rate through 1992, and research and development as a percentage of the industry's sales revenue remains roughly 40 percent higher than early 1980s levels. Labor productivity soared at an impressive 16 percent annual rate during the same period and has risen even more over the last two years.

The results speak for themselves. With the aid of the Semiconductor Agreement (which was renewed in 1991 and remains in place), sales of foreign chips in Japan edged above 20 percent in late 1993 and currently are just below that threshold. U.S. merchant chips continue to account for some 90 percent of these increased foreign sales. By 1991, U.S. merchant producers held 50 percent of the world semiconductor market outside the still largely closed Japanese market. By 1992 U.S.-based companies had moved into a tie with their Japan-based competitors in the world semiconductor production race, and they maintained a small lead in 1993. Just as important, U.S. producers introduced scores of innovative products to world markets. And producer prices for the industry increased only 4 percent between 1982 and 1991—less than one-fourth the rise for all manufacturing. Since 1986, when the Semiconductor Agreement was negotiated, producer prices in the industry have actually fallen slightly.

TEXTILES AND APPAREL

SINCE THE LATE 1950S, the American textile and apparel industries have received various forms of import relief. And since 1974, world trade in these sectors has been governed by the Multifiber Arrangement (MFA), which seeks to prevent disruptive floods of textiles and apparel into the world's major consuming countries by establishing quotas for the world's exporting countries.

The MFA, however, is hardly an impregnable trade barrier. The quotas for exporters—principally low-wage Third World producers such as China and India—must be increased every year. Currently, they stand so high that many exporting countries have trouble filling them. Further, no provisions exist for reciprocity; thus Third World exporters are required to import virtually nothing. The result is import penetration levels that have reached 44 percent for the two industries combined. The MFA will be phased out in ten years because of the GATT accord, despite the failure of U.S. negotiators to get significant foreign market access at the Uruguay Round talks.

Nonetheless, the last decade or more has seen a frenetic modernization by U.S. textile and apparel companies. Annual new capital expenditures for textile mill products have climbed in real terms from $1.6 billion in 1980 to nearly $2.5 billion in 1993, financing major purchases of electronically monitored looms and other new equipment. Industry-financed research and development increased from $116 million in 1981 to $210 million in 1988. And productivity shot up by more than 77 percent between 1980 and 1992. On the management end, U.S. textile companies introduced many new fabrics and fibers and shortened production cycles significantly. Meanwhile, since 1982, producer prices for textiles have risen only 16.3 percent, just under the

16.5 percent figure for all industrial commodities. Free trade advocates are entitled to ask why the textile and apparel industries began their modernization campaigns well after the MFA was implemented. In response, advocates of import relief are entitled to ask why, in direct contradiction of free-trade ideology, these industries launched and sustained significant modernization while enjoying import relief.

A THEORY FULL OF HOLES

WHY HAS THE conventional wisdom of free trade been so wrong? Three gaping holes in its theoretical foundations are partly responsible. First, economic theorists ignore common business sense. Declining investment in declining industries is no mystery, and certainly no sign of moral turpitude. Rather, it is the only intelligent response for an industrialist whose government has ignored the threats from abroad posed by dumping, protected foreign markets and subsidized competition and who faces macroeconomic, tax and regulatory policies at home that have dramatically eroded the economy's capacity to create wealth and reduced incentives to save and invest.

Import relief measures helped convince industries that they were not stuck with trying to buck impossible odds, competing unaided in a world in which free-trade principles are too often honored in the breach. Import relief programs signaled to executives that their industries could indeed have a future and that retooling stood a real chance of being rewarded. Further, import relief often helped firms amass the finances to make investments that would bolster their bottom lines and ultimately improve their access to capital markets.

Second, economists overlook one of their most venerable concepts—the infant industry phenomenon. Since Adam Smith's day even the most ardent laissez-faire champions have recognized that import relief can be essential to helping new companies break into the markets of long-established industries, establish market share abroad and get a leg up on competitors in new industries. Both nineteenth-century America and post-World War II Japan nurtured infant industries skillfully enough to become economic superpowers.

Today, laissez-faire theory still seems to accept the value of sheltering infant industries, but only when implemented by Third World countries (presumably because they stand at the bottom of the economic ladder). But this rule of thumb may be obsolete because of the distinctive nature of modern industry and advanced technology. As pointed out by Edward Luttwak, fundamentally new technologies and manufacturing processes now emerge so rapidly and product cycles are so short (even in long-established sectors such as steel and textiles) that the functional equivalents of infant industries may be springing up in developed and developing countries alike. Thus a commonsensible modification of well-established economic theory indicates that import relief could give even competitive, established industries the time and resources needed to innovate continually and remain competitive. This breathing space is even more important when competitors are protected or subsidized.

Third, theorists have ruled out the possibility that public policymakers could ever be smart enough to develop import relief programs that give industry a realistic chance to survive and at the same time keep the competitive pressure on. The steel VERs, for example, were explicitly linked to industry modernization and retraining efforts. Likewise, the MFA has set quotas for textile and apparel imports, but the quotas expand every year.

A REALISTIC JOBS CALCULUS

ANOTHER MAJOR reason U.S. policymakers have not adequately employed import relief programs, despite their proven success, is the alleged cost of these programs to consumers and taxpayers. Laissez-faire advocates insist that, whatever their benefits to industry, all tariffs and quotas are unacceptable because they preserve particular American jobs at an exorbitant cost to all taxpayers and consumers. One recent, widely quoted study by the laissez-faire-oriented Institute for International Economics (IIE), titled *Measuring the Costs of Protection in the United States*, pegs the cost to American consumers of such U.S. trade barriers at $70 billion in 1990. According to laissez-faire thinking, the resources spent on keeping workers employed by uncompetitive industries could be better spent by the public or private sector on promoting economic activity in fields where Americans have clearer comparative advantages.

Yet the studies behind these arguments tend to examine the costs and benefits of job preservation selectively. They typically include costs that have little to do with sheltering industries and workers that are incapable of competing in open international markets, and they ignore many of the efficiency and output gains from maintaining employment that would otherwise be threatened.

The IIE study is a case in point. For instance, more than 40 percent of the estimated $70 billion cost of protection is derived from tariffs that have been part of the world trading system for decades. Not only have these tariffs fallen to very low levels (two to three percent on average), but their main purpose is often raising revenue. They should not be counted as expenditures for job protection. In addition, many of the U.S. policies and laws that preserve American jobs were instituted to offset predatory foreign trade practices, such as heavy subsidies and dumping, that give foreign producers major advantages in American and global markets and have nothing to do with levels of economic competitiveness.

> Washington has designed import relief programs intelligently.

Moreover, the IIE authors themselves recognized that the $70 billion figure is a gross figure. Acknowledging that most of the added consumer costs remain in the United States (either as higher profits for domestic producers or added tax revenues from tariffs) they estimate the net cost of protection to be a mere $11 billion—a drop in the bucket in a $6 trillion economy. And even this figure is dubious. Additional economic costs caused by import relief are no doubt incurred from the misallocation of some resources, but the authors ignore a much broader range of benefits. These include the savings on adjustment costs for workers who would have lost their jobs without import relief, the added new investment that would be required to employ them in other industries, the potential benefits to productivity if the domestic producers and the federal government use their added profits and tariff revenues to finance new private and public investment, and the long-term output and technology benefits of saving an industry threatened with destruction.

Ironically, many of the economists who rail against import relief on principle support various other measures that exact considerable consumer costs: consumption taxes, oil import fees or gasoline taxes, and exchange-rate management. In these cases, they understand that goals other than short-term consumer welfare, such as higher national savings rates or greater energy security, often deserve national support. But when the trade-off involves balancing the goal of lower consumer prices against the goals of boosting employment, preserving communities dependent on certain industries or holding down welfare rolls, these economists turn a blind eye.

WALL-TO-WALL ECONOMY

IMPORT RELIEF is like any other public policy. It is neither inherently good nor inherently bad. It can be done well or it can be done poorly. Contrary to the predictions of laissez-faire ideologues who claim that government can do nothing right, or that government support for business inevitably degenerates into an endless exercise in pork-barreling, Washington has in recent years designed import relief programs intelligently, with just the right combination of carrots and sticks needed to give threatened industries a second chance. Contrary to the predictions of business bashers, American corporations have not tried to remain on the dole indefinitely, and have usually not viewed import relief as an opportunity to sit back and fatten their coffers at consumer and taxpayer expense. Instead, they have worked overtime and spent vast sums to reinvent themselves. Not all of the energy or money was wisely spent, but the effort was made, and all five industries examined have scored major successes. Import relief is no panacea for America's economic ills. But if one examines the facts, instead of the dogma, it will be seen as an essential component of a comprehensive approach to boosting competitiveness. ❧

The Myth of Asia's Miracle

Paul Krugman

A CAUTIONARY FABLE

ONCE UPON a time, Western opinion leaders found themselves both impressed and frightened by the extraordinary growth rates achieved by a set of Eastern economies. Although those economies were still substantially poorer and smaller than those of the West, the speed with which they had transformed themselves from peasant societies into industrial powerhouses, their continuing ability to achieve growth rates several times higher than the advanced nations, and their increasing ability to challenge or even surpass American and European technology in certain areas seemed to call into question the dominance not only of Western power but of Western ideology. The leaders of those nations did not share our faith in free markets or unlimited civil liberties. They asserted with increasing self-confidence that their system was superior: societies that accepted strong, even authoritarian governments and were willing to limit individual liberties in the interest of the common good, take charge of their economies, and sacrifice short-run consumer interests for the sake of long-run growth would eventually outperform the increasingly chaotic societies of the West. And a growing minority of Western intellectuals agreed.

The gap between Western and Eastern economic performance eventually became a political issue. The Democrats recaptured the White House under the leadership of a young, energetic new presi-

---

PAUL KRUGMAN is Professor of Economics at Stanford University. His most recent book is *Peddling Prosperity: Economic Sense and Nonsense in the Age of Diminished Expectations*.

dent who pledged to "get the country moving again"—a pledge that, to him and his closest advisers, meant accelerating America's economic growth to meet the Eastern challenge.

The time, of course, was the early 1960s. The dynamic young president was John F. Kennedy. The technological feats that so alarmed the West were the launch of Sputnik and the early Soviet lead in space. And the rapidly growing Eastern economies were those of the Soviet Union and its satellite nations.

While the growth of communist economies was the subject of innumerable alarmist books and polemical articles in the 1950s, some economists who looked seriously at the roots of that growth were putting together a picture that differed substantially from most popular assumptions. Communist growth rates were certainly impressive, but not magical. The rapid growth in output could be fully explained by rapid growth in inputs: expansion of employment, increases in education levels, and, above all, massive investment in physical capital. Once those inputs were taken into account, the growth in output was unsurprising—or, to put it differently, the big surprise about Soviet growth was that when closely examined it posed no mystery.

This economic analysis had two crucial implications. First, most of the speculation about the superiority of the communist system—including the popular view that Western economies could painlessly accelerate their own growth by borrowing some aspects of that system—was off base. Rapid Soviet economic growth was based entirely on one attribute: the willingness to save, to sacrifice current consumption for the sake of future production. The communist example offered no hint of a free lunch.

Second, the economic analysis of communist countries' growth implied some future limits to their industrial expansion—in other words, implied that a naive projection of their past growth rates into the future was likely to greatly overstate their real prospects. Economic growth that is based on expansion of inputs, rather than on growth in output per unit of input, is inevitably subject to diminishing returns. It was simply not possible for the Soviet economies to sustain the rates of growth of labor force participation, average education levels, and above all the physical capital stock that had prevailed in previous years. Communist growth would predictably slow down, perhaps drastically.

Can there really be any parallel between the growth of Warsaw Pact nations in the 1950s and the spectacular Asian growth that now preoccupies policy intellectuals? At some levels, of course, the parallel is far-fetched: Singapore in the 1990s does not look much like the Soviet Union in the 1950s, and Singapore's Lee Kuan Yew bears little resemblance to the U.S.S.R.'s Nikita Khrushchev and less to Joseph Stalin. Yet the results of recent economic research into the sources of Pacific Rim growth give the few people who recall the great debate over Soviet growth a strong sense of déjà vu. Now, as then, the contrast between popular hype and realistic prospects, between conventional wisdom and hard numbers, remains so great that sensible economic analysis is not only widely ignored, but when it does get aired, it is usually dismissed as grossly implausible.

Popular enthusiasm about Asia's boom deserves to have some cold water thrown on it. Rapid Asian growth is less of a model for the West than many writers claim, and the future prospects for that growth are more limited than almost anyone now imagines. Any such assault on almost universally held beliefs must, of course, overcome a barrier of incredulity. This article began with a disguised account of the Soviet growth debate of 30 years ago to try to gain a hearing for the proposition that we may be revisiting an old error. We have been here before. The problem with this literary device, however, is that so few people now remember how impressive and terrifying the Soviet empire's economic performance once seemed. Before turning to Asian growth, then, it may be useful to review an important but largely forgotten piece of economic history.

'WE WILL BURY YOU'

LIVING IN a world strewn with the wreckage of the Soviet empire, it is hard for most people to realize that there was a time when the Soviet economy, far from being a byword for the failure of socialism, was one of the wonders of the world—that when Khrushchev pounded his shoe on the U.N. podium and declared, "We will bury you," it was an economic rather than a military boast. It is therefore a shock to browse through, say, issues of *Foreign Affairs* from the mid-1950s through the early 1960s and discover that at least one article a year dealt with the implications of growing Soviet industrial might.

Illustrative of the tone of discussion was a 1957 article by Calvin B. Hoover.[1] Like many Western economists, Hoover criticized official Soviet statistics, arguing that they exaggerated the true growth rate. Nonetheless, he concluded that Soviet claims of astonishing achievement were fully justified: their economy was achieving a rate of growth "twice as high as that attained by any important capitalistic country over any considerable number of years [and] three times as high as the average annual rate of increase in the United States." He concluded that it was probable that "a collectivist, authoritarian state" was inherently better at achieving economic growth than free-market democracies and projected that the Soviet economy might outstrip that of the United States by the early 1970s.

These views were not considered outlandish at the time. On the contrary, the general image of Soviet central planning was that it might be brutal, and might not do a very good job of providing consumer goods, but that it was very effective at promoting industrial growth. In 1960 Wassily Leontief described the Soviet economy as being "directed with determined ruthless skill"—and did so without supporting argument, confident he was expressing a view shared by his readers.

Yet many economists studying Soviet growth were gradually coming to a very different conclusion. Although they did not dispute the fact of past Soviet growth, they offered a new interpretation of the nature of that growth, one that implied a reconsideration of future

---

[1] Hoover's tone—critical of Soviet data but nonetheless accepting the fact of extraordinary achievement—was typical of much of the commentary of the time (see, for example, a series of articles in *The Atlantic Monthly* by Edward Crankshaw, beginning with "Soviet Industry" in the November 1955 issue). Anxiety about the political implications of Soviet growth reached its high-water mark in 1959, the year Khrushchev visited America. *Newsweek* took Khrushchev's boasts seriously enough to warn that the Soviet Union might well be "on the high road to economic domination of the world." And in hearings held by the Joint Economic Committee late that year, CIA Director Allen Dulles warned, "If the Soviet industrial growth rate persists at eight or nine percent per annum over the next decade, as is forecast, the gap between our two economies . . . will be dangerously narrowed."

The Soviet miracle: perspiration, not inspiration

Soviet prospects. To understand this reinterpretation, it is necessary to make a brief detour into economic theory to discuss a seemingly abstruse, but in fact intensely practical, concept: growth accounting.

ACCOUNTING FOR THE SOVIET SLOWDOWN

IT IS A TAUTOLOGY that economic expansion represents the sum of two sources of growth. On one side are increases in "inputs": growth in employment, in the education level of workers, and in the stock of physical capital (machines, buildings, roads, and so on). On the other side are increases in the output per unit of input; such increases may result from better management or better economic policy, but in the long run are primarily due to increases in knowledge.

The basic idea of growth accounting is to give life to this formula by calculating explicit measures of both. The accounting can then tell us how much of growth is due to each input—say, capital as opposed to labor—and how much is due to increased efficiency.

We all do a primitive form of growth accounting every time we talk about labor productivity; in so doing we are implicitly distinguishing between the part of overall national growth due to the growth in the supply of labor and the part due to an increase in the value of goods produced by the average worker. Increases in labor productivity, however, are not always caused by the increased efficiency of workers. Labor is only one of a number of inputs; workers may produce more, not because they are better managed or have more technological knowledge, but simply because they have better machinery. A man with a bulldozer can dig a ditch faster than one with only a shovel, but he is not more efficient; he just has more capital to work with. The aim of growth accounting is to produce an index that combines all measurable inputs and to measure the rate of growth of national income relative to that index—to estimate what is known as "total factor productivity."[2]

So far this may seem like a purely academic exercise. As soon as one starts to think in terms of growth accounting, however, one arrives at a crucial insight about the process of economic growth: sustained growth in a nation's per capita income can only occur if there is a rise in output *per unit of input.*[3]

Mere increases in inputs, without an increase in the efficiency with which those inputs are used—investing in more machinery and infrastructure—must run into diminishing returns; input-driven growth is inevitably limited.

How, then, have today's advanced nations been able to achieve sustained growth in per capita income over the past 150 years? The

---

[2] At first, creating an index of all inputs may seem like comparing apples and oranges, that is, trying to add together noncomparable items like the hours a worker puts in and the cost of the new machine he uses. How does one determine the weights for the different components? The economists' answer is to use market returns. If the average worker earns $15 an hour, give each person-hour in the index a weight of $15; if a machine that costs $100,000 on average earns $10,000 in profits each year (a 10 percent rate of return), then give each such machine a weight of $10,000; and so on.

[3] To see why, let's consider a hypothetical example. To keep matters simple, let's assume that the country has a stationary population and labor force, so that all increases in the investment in machinery, etc., raise the amount of capital per worker in the country. Let us finally make up some arbitrary numbers. Specifically, let us assume that initially each worker is equipped with $10,000 worth of equipment; that each worker produces goods and services worth $10,000; and that capital initially earns a 40 percent rate of return, that is, each $10,000 of machinery earns annual profits of $4,000. (*Cont'd.*)

answer is that technological advances have led to a continual increase in total factor productivity—a continual rise in national income for each unit of input. In a famous estimate, MIT Professor Robert Solow concluded that technological progress has accounted for 80 percent of the long-term rise in U.S. per capita income, with increased investment in capital explaining only the remaining 20 percent.

When economists began to study the growth of the Soviet economy, they did so using the tools of growth accounting. Of course, Soviet data posed some problems. Not only was it hard to piece together usable estimates of output and input (Raymond Powell, a Yale professor, wrote that the job "in many ways resembled an archaeological dig"), but there were philosophical difficulties as well. In a socialist economy one could hardly measure capital input using market returns, so researchers were forced to impute returns based on those in market economies at similar levels of development. Still, when the efforts began, researchers were pretty sure about what they would find. Just as capitalist growth had been based on growth in both inputs and efficiency, with efficiency the main source of rising per capita income, they expected to find that rapid Soviet growth reflected both rapid input growth and rapid growth in efficiency.

But what they actually found was that Soviet growth was based on

---

(*Cont'd.*) Suppose, now, that this country consistently invests 20 percent of its output, that is, uses 20 percent of its income to add to its capital stock. How rapidly will the economy grow?

Initially, very fast indeed. In the first year, the capital stock per worker will rise by 20 percent of $10,000, that is, by $2,000. At a 40 percent rate of return, that will increase output by $800: an 8 percent rate of growth.

But this high rate of growth will not be sustainable. Consider the situation of the economy by the time that capital per worker has doubled to $20,000. First, output per worker will not have increased in the same proportion, because capital stock is only one input. Even with the additions to capital stock up to that point achieving a 40 percent rate of return, output per worker will have increased only to $14,000. And the rate of return is also certain to decline—say to 30 or even 25 percent. (One bulldozer added to a construction project can make a huge difference to productivity. By the time a dozen are on-site, one more may not make that much difference.) The combination of those factors means that if the investment share of output is the same, the growth rate will sharply decline. Taking 20 percent of $14,000 gives us $2,800; at a 30 percent rate of return, this will raise output by only $840, that is, generate a growth rate of only 6 percent; at a 25 percent rate of return it will generate a growth rate of only 5 percent. As capital continues to accumulate, the rate of return and hence the rate of growth will continue to decline.

rapid growth in inputs—end of story. The rate of efficiency growth was not only unspectacular, it was well below the rates achieved in Western economies. Indeed, by some estimates, it was virtually nonexistent.[4]

The immense Soviet efforts to mobilize economic resources were hardly news. Stalinist planners had moved millions of workers from farms to cities, pushed millions of women into the labor force and millions of men into longer hours, pursued massive programs of education, and above all plowed an ever-growing proportion of the country's industrial output back into the construction of new factories. Still, the big surprise was that once one had taken the effects of these more or less measurable inputs into account, there was nothing left to explain. The most shocking thing about Soviet growth was its comprehensibility.

This comprehensibility implied two crucial conclusions. First, claims about the superiority of planned over market economies turned out to be based on a misapprehension. If the Soviet economy had a special strength, it was its ability to mobilize resources, not its ability to use them efficiently. It was obvious to everyone that the Soviet Union in 1960 was much less efficient than the United States. The surprise was that it showed no signs of closing the gap.

Second, because input-driven growth is an inherently limited process, Soviet growth was virtually certain to slow down. Long before the slowing of Soviet growth became obvious, it was predicted on the basis of growth accounting. (Economists did not predict the implosion of the Soviet economy a generation later, but that is a whole different problem.)

It's an interesting story and a useful cautionary tale about the dangers of naive extrapolation of past trends. But is it relevant to the modern world?

PAPER TIGERS

AT FIRST, it is hard to see anything in common between the Asian success stories of recent years and the Soviet Union of three decades

---

[4] This work was summarized by Raymond Powell, "Economic Growth in the U.S.S.R.," *Scientific American*, December 1968.

ago. Indeed, it is safe to say that the typical business traveler to, say, Singapore, ensconced in one of that city's gleaming hotels, never even thinks of any parallel to its roach-infested counterparts in Moscow. How can the slick exuberance of the Asian boom be compared with the Soviet Union's grim drive to industrialize?

And yet there are surprising similarities. The newly industrializing countries of Asia, like the Soviet Union of the 1950s, have achieved rapid growth in large part through an astonishing mobilization of resources. Once one accounts for the role of rapidly growing inputs in these countries' growth, one finds little left to explain. Asian growth, like that of the Soviet Union in its high-growth era, seems to be driven by extraordinary growth in inputs like labor and capital rather than by gains in efficiency.[5]

Consider, in particular, the case of Singapore. Between 1966 and 1990, the Singaporean economy grew a remarkable 8.5 percent per annum, three times as fast as the United States; per capita income grew at a 6.6 percent rate, roughly doubling every decade. This achievement seems to be a kind of economic miracle. But the miracle turns out to have been based on perspiration rather than inspiration: Singapore grew through a mobilization of resources that would have done Stalin proud. The employed share of the population surged from 27 to 51 percent. The educational standards of that work force were dramatically upgraded: while in 1966 more than half the workers had no formal education at all, by 1990 two-thirds had completed secondary education. Above all, the country had made an awesome investment in physical capital: investment as a

---

[5] There have been a number of recent efforts to quantify the sources of rapid growth in the Pacific Rim. Key readings include two papers by Professor Lawrence Lau of Stanford University and his associate Jong-Il Kim, "The Sources of Growth of the East Asian Newly Industrialized Countries," *Journal of the Japanese and International Economies*, 1994, and "The Role of Human Capital in the Economic Growth of the East Asian Newly Industrialized Countries," mimeo, Stanford University, 1993; and three papers by Professor Alwyn Young, a rising star in growth economics, "A Tale of Two Cities: Factor Accumulation and Technical Change in Hong Kong and Singapore," *NBER Macroeconomics Annual 1992*, MIT Press; "Lessons from the East Asian NICS: A Contrarian View," *European Economic Review Papers and Proceedings*, May 1994; and "The Tyranny of Numbers: Confronting the Statistical Realities of the East Asian Growth Experience," NBER Working Paper No. 4680, March 1994.

share of output rose from 11 to more than 40 percent.[6]

Even without going through the formal exercise of growth accounting, these numbers should make it obvious that Singapore's growth has been based largely on one-time changes in behavior that cannot be repeated. Over the past generation the percentage of people employed has almost doubled; it cannot double again. A half-educated work force has been replaced by one in which the bulk of workers has high school diplomas; it is unlikely that a generation from now most Singaporeans will have Ph.D.s. And an investment share of 40 percent is amazingly high by any standard; a share of 70 percent would be ridiculous. So one can immediately conclude that Singapore is unlikely to achieve future growth rates comparable to those of the past.

But it is only when one actually does the quantitative accounting that the astonishing result emerges: all of Singapore's growth can be explained by increases in measured inputs. There is no sign at all of increased efficiency. In this sense, the growth of Lee Kuan Yew's Singapore is an economic twin of the growth of Stalin's Soviet Union—growth achieved purely through mobilization of resources. Of course, Singapore today is far more prosperous than the U.S.S.R. ever was—even at its peak in the Brezhnev years—because Singapore is closer to, though still below, the efficiency of Western economies. The point, however, is that Singapore's economy has always been relatively efficient; it just used to be starved of capital and educated workers.

Singapore's case is admittedly the most extreme. Other rapidly growing East Asian economies have not increased their labor force participation as much, made such dramatic improvements in educational levels, or raised investment rates quite as far. Nonetheless, the basic conclusion is the same: there is startlingly little evidence of improvements in efficiency. Kim and Lau conclude of the four Asian "tigers" that "the hypothesis that there has been no technical progress during the postwar period cannot be rejected for the four East Asian newly industrialized countries." Young, more poetically, notes that once one allows for

---

[6] These figures are taken from Young, *ibid.* Although foreign corporations have played an important role in Singapore's economy, the great bulk of investment in Singapore, as in all of the newly industrialized East Asian economies, has been financed out of domestic savings.

their rapid growth of inputs, the productivity performance of the "tigers" falls "from the heights of Olympus to the plains of Thessaly."

This conclusion runs so counter to conventional wisdom that it is extremely difficult for the economists who have reached it to get a hearing. As early as 1982 a Harvard graduate student, Yuan Tsao, found little evidence of efficiency growth in her dissertation on Singapore, but her work was, as Young puts it, "ignored or dismissed as unbelievable." When Kim and Lau presented their work at a 1992 conference in Taipei, it received a more respectful hearing, but had little immediate impact But when Young tried to make the case for input-driven Asian growth at the 1993 meetings of the European Economic Association, he was met with a stone wall of disbelief.

In Young's most recent paper there is an evident tone of exasperation with this insistence on clinging to the conventional wisdom in the teeth of the evidence. He titles the paper "The Tyranny of Numbers"—by which he means that you may not want to believe this, buster, but there's just no way around the data. He begins with an ironic introduction, written in a deadpan, Sergeant Friday, "Just the facts, ma'am" style: "This is a fairly boring and tedious paper, and is intentionally so. This paper provides no new interpretations of the East Asian experience to interest the historian, derives no new theoretical implications of the forces behind the East Asian growth process to motivate the theorist, and draws no new policy implications from the subtleties of East Asian government intervention to excite the policy activist. Instead, this paper concentrates its energies on providing a careful analysis of the historical patterns of output growth, factor accumulation, and productivity growth in the newly industrializing countries of East Asia."

Of course, he is being disingenuous. His conclusion undermines most of the conventional wisdom about the future role of Asian nations in the world economy and, as a consequence, in international politics. But readers will have noticed that the statistical analysis that puts such a different interpretation on Asian growth focuses on the "tigers," the relatively small countries to whom the name "newly industrializing countries" was first applied. But what about the large countries? What about Japan and China?

THE GREAT JAPANESE GROWTH SLOWDOWN

MANY PEOPLE who are committed to the view that the destiny of
the world economy lies with the Pacific Rim are likely to counter
skepticism about East Asian growth prospects with the example of
Japan. Here, after all, is a country that started out poor and has now
become the second-largest industrial power. Why doubt that other
Asian nations can do the same?

There are two answers to that question. First, while many authors
have written of an "Asian system"—a common denominator that
underlies all of the Asian success stories—the statistical evidence tells
a different story. Japan's growth in the 1950s and 1960s does not resem-
ble Singapore's growth in the 1970s and 1980s. Japan, unlike the East
Asian "tigers," seems to have grown both through high rates of input
growth and through high rates of efficiency growth. Today's fast-
growth economies are nowhere near converging on U.S. efficiency
levels, but Japan is staging an unmistakable technological catch-up.

Second, while Japan's historical performance has indeed been
remarkable, the era of miraculous Japanese growth now lies well in the
past. Most years Japan still manages to grow faster than the other
advanced nations, but that gap in growth rates is now far smaller than
it used to be, and is shrinking.

The story of the great Japanese growth slowdown has been oddly
absent from the vast polemical literature on Japan and its role in the
world economy. Much of that literature seems stuck in a time warp,
with authors writing as if Japan were still the miracle growth economy of the 1960s and early 1970s. Granted, the severe recession that
has gripped Japan since 1991 will end soon if it has not done so already,
and the Japanese economy will probably stage a vigorous short-term
recovery. The point, however, is that even a full recovery will only
reach a level that is far below what many sensible observers predicted
20 years ago.

It may be useful to compare Japan's growth prospects as they
appeared 20 years ago and as they appear now. In 1973 Japan was still
a substantially smaller and poorer economy than the United States.
Its per capita GDP was only 55 percent of America's, while its overall

GDP was only 27 percent as large. But the rapid growth of the Japanese economy clearly portended a dramatic change. Over the previous decade Japan's real GDP had grown at a torrid 8.9 percent annually, with per capita output growing at a 7.7 percent rate. Although American growth had been high by its own historical standards, at 3.9 percent (2.7 percent per capita) it was not in the same league. Clearly, the Japanese were rapidly gaining on us.

In fact, a straightforward projection of these trends implied that a major reversal of positions lay not far in the future. At the growth rate of 1963-73, Japan would overtake the United States in real per capita income by 1985, and total Japanese output would exceed that of the United States by 1998! At the time, people took such trend projections very seriously indeed. One need only look at the titles of such influential books as Herman Kahn's *The Emerging Japanese Superstate* or Ezra Vogel's *Japan as Number One* to remember that Japan appeared, to many observers, to be well on its way to global economic dominance.

Well, it has not happened, at least not so far. Japan has indeed continued to rise in the economic rankings, but at a far more modest pace than those projections suggested. In 1992 Japan's per capita income was still only 83 percent of the United States', and its overall output was only 42 percent of the American level. The reason was that growth from 1973 to 1992 was far slower than in the high-growth years: GDP grew only 3.7 percent annually, and GDP per capita grew only 3 percent per year. The United States also experienced a growth slowdown after 1973, but it was not nearly as drastic.

If one projects those post-1973 growth rates into the future, one still sees a relative Japanese rise, but a far less dramatic one. Following 1973-92 trends, Japan's per capita income will outstrip that of the United States in 2002; its overall output does not exceed America's until the year 2047. Even this probably overestimates Japanese prospects. Japanese economists generally believe that their country's rate of growth of potential output, the rate that it will be able to sustain once it has taken up the slack left by the recession, is now no more than three percent. And that rate is achieved only through a very high rate of investment, nearly twice as high a share of GDP as in the United States. When one takes into account the growing evidence for

The Myth of Asia's Miracle

at least a modest acceleration of U.S. productivity growth in the last few years, one ends up with the probable conclusion that Japanese efficiency is gaining on that of the United States at a snail's pace, if at all, and there is the distinct possibility that per capita income in Japan may never overtake that in America. In other words, Japan is not quite as overwhelming an example of economic prowess as is sometimes thought, and in any case Japan's experience has much less in common with that of other Asian nations than is generally imagined.

THE CHINA SYNDROME

FOR THE skeptic, the case of China poses much greater difficulties about Asian destiny than that of Japan. Although China is still a very poor country, its population is so huge that it will become a major economic power if it achieves even a fraction of Western productivity levels. And China, unlike Japan, has in recent years posted truly impressive rates of economic growth. What about its future prospects?

Accounting for China's boom is difficult for both practical and philosophical reasons. The practical problem is that while we know that China is growing very rapidly, the quality of the numbers is extremely poor. It was recently revealed that official Chinese statistics on foreign investment have been overstated by as much as a factor of six. The reason was that the government offers tax and regulatory incentives to foreign investors, providing an incentive for domestic entrepreneurs to invent fictitious foreign partners or to work through foreign fronts. This episode hardly inspires confidence in any other statistic that emanates from that dynamic but awesomely corrupt society.

The philosophical problem is that it is unclear what year to use as a baseline. If one measures Chinese growth from the point at which it made a decisive turn toward the market, say 1978, there is little question that there has been dramatic improvement in efficiency as well as rapid growth in inputs. But it is hardly surprising that a major recovery in economic efficiency occurred as the country emerged from the chaos of Mao Zedong's later years. If one instead measures growth from before the Cultural Revolution, say 1964, the picture looks more like the East Asian "tigers": only modest growth in efficiency, with most growth driven by inputs. This calculation, however, also seems unfair: one is weighing down the buoyant performance of Chinese capitalism with the leaden performance of Chinese socialism. Perhaps we should simply split the difference: guess that some, but not all, of the efficiency gains since the turn toward the market represent a one-time recovery, while the rest represent a sustainable trend.

Even a modest slowing in China's growth will change the geopolitical outlook substantially. The World Bank estimates that the Chinese economy is currently about 40 percent as large as that of the United States. Suppose that the U.S. economy continues to grow at 2.5 percent each year. If China can continue to grow at 10 percent annually, by the year 2010 its economy will be a third larger than ours. But if Chinese growth is only a more realistic 7 percent, its GDP will be only 82 percent of that of the United States. There will still be a substantial shift of the world's economic center of gravity, but it will be far less drastic than many people now imagine.

THE MYSTERY THAT WASN'T

THE EXTRAORDINARY record of economic growth in the newly industrializing countries of East Asia has powerfully influenced the conventional wisdom about both economic policy and geopolitics. Many, perhaps most, writers on the global economy now take it for granted that the success of these economies demonstrates three propositions. First, there is a major diffusion of world technology in progress, and Western nations are losing their traditional advantage. Second, the world's economic center of gravity will inevitably shift to the Asian nations of the western Pacific. Third, in what is perhaps a minority view, Asian successes demonstrate the superiority of economies with fewer civil liberties and more planning than we in the West have been willing to accept.

All three conclusions are called into question by the simple observation that the remarkable record of East Asian growth has been matched by input growth so rapid that Asian economic growth, incredibly, ceases to be a mystery.

Consider first the assertion that the advanced countries are losing their technological advantage. A heavy majority of recent tracts on the world economy have taken it as self-evident that technology now increasingly flows across borders, and that newly industrializing nations are increasingly able to match the productivity of more established economies. Many writers warn that this diffusion of technology will place huge strains on Western society as capital flows to the Third World and imports from those nations undermine the West's industrial base.

There are severe conceptual problems with this scenario even if its initial premise is right.[7] But in any case, while technology may have diffused within particular industries, the available evidence provides absolutely no justification for the view that overall world technological gaps are vanishing. On the contrary, Kim and Lau find "no apparent convergence between the technologies" of the newly industrialized nations and the established industrial powers; Young finds that the rates in the growth of efficiency in the East Asian "tigers" are no higher than those in many advanced nations.

The absence of any dramatic convergence in technology helps explain what would otherwise be a puzzle: in spite of a great deal of rhetoric about North-South capital movement, actual capital flows to developing countries in the 1990s have so far been very small—and they have primarily gone to Latin America, not East Asia. Indeed, several of the East Asian "tigers" have recently become significant exporters of capital. This behavior would be extremely odd if these economies, which still pay wages well below advanced-country levels, were rapidly achieving advanced-country productivity. It is, however, perfectly reasonable if growth in East Asia has been primarily input-driven, and if the capital piling up there is beginning to yield diminishing returns.

If growth in East Asia is indeed running into diminishing returns, however, the conventional wisdom about an Asian-centered world economy needs some rethinking. It would be a mistake to overstate this case: barring a catastrophic political upheaval, it is likely that

---

[7] See Paul Krugman, "Does Third World Growth Hurt First World Prosperity?" *Harvard Business Review*, July 1994.

growth in East Asia will continue to outpace growth in the West for the next decade and beyond. But it will not do so at the pace of recent years. From the perspective of the year 2010, current projections of Asian supremacy extrapolated from recent trends may well look almost as silly as 1960s-vintage forecasts of Soviet industrial supremacy did from the perspective of the Brezhnev years.

Finally, the realities of East Asian growth suggest that we may have to unlearn some popular lessons. It has become common to assert that East Asian economic success demonstrates the fallacy of our traditional laissez-faire approach to economic policy and that the growth of these economies shows the effectiveness of sophisticated industrial policies and selective protectionism. Authors such as James Fallows have asserted that the nations of that region have evolved a common "Asian system," whose lessons we ignore at our peril. The extremely diverse institutions and policies of the various newly industrialized Asian countries, let alone Japan, cannot really be called a common system. But in any case, if Asian success reflects the benefits of strategic trade and industrial policies, those benefits should surely be manifested in an unusual and impressive rate of growth in the efficiency of the economy. And there is no sign of such exceptional efficiency growth.

The newly industrializing countries of the Pacific Rim have received a reward for their extraordinary mobilization of resources that is no more than what the most boringly conventional economic theory would lead us to expect. If there is a secret to Asian growth, it is simply deferred gratification, the willingness to sacrifice current satisfaction for future gain.

That's a hard answer to accept, especially for those American policy intellectuals who recoil from the dreary task of reducing deficits and raising the national savings rate. But economics is not a dismal science because the economists like it that way; it is because in the end we must submit to the tyranny not just of the numbers, but of the logic they express. ☯